BIBLICAL STEWARDSHIP

TIME, TALENTS, TREASURES, RELATIONSHIPS, MINISTRY

DR. PATRICK R. BRINEY

Biblical Stewardship:
Time, Talents, Treasures, Relationships, Ministry

Patrick R. Briney
patrickbriney.com

Published by Life Changing Scriptures
lifechangingscriptures.org

CONTENTS

1

WHAT DOES JESUS CONSIDER GOOD STEWARDSHIP TO BE?

Jesus told a story about three stewards who were entrusted with the care of their Lord's possessions. In Matthew 25:14–30, Jesus said,

For the kingdom of heaven is as a man travelling into a far country, who called his own servants, and delivered unto them his goods.

And unto one he gave five talents, to another two, and to another one; to every man according to his several ability; and straightway took his journey. Then he that had received the five talents went and traded with the same, and made them other five talents. And likewise he that had received two, he also gained other two. But he that had received one went and digged in the earth, and hid his lord's money.

After a long time the lord of those servants cometh, and reckoneth with them.

And so he that had received five talents came and brought other five talents, saying, Lord, thou deliveredst unto me five talents: behold, I have gained beside them five talents more. His lord said unto him, Well done, thou good and faithful servant: thou hast been faithful over a few

things, I will make thee ruler over many things: enter thou into the joy of thy lord.

He also that had received two talents came and said, Lord, thou deliveredst unto me two talents: behold, I have gained two other talents beside them. His lord said unto him, Well done, good and faithful servant; thou hast been faithful over a few things, I will make thee ruler over many things: enter thou into the joy of thy lord.

Then he which had received the one talent came and said, Lord, I knew thee that thou art an hard man, reaping where thou hast not sown, and gathering where thou hast not strawed: And I was afraid, and went and hid thy talent in the earth: lo, there thou hast that is thine. His lord answered and said unto him, Thou wicked and slothful servant, thou knewest that I reap where I sowed not, and gather where I have not strawed: Thou oughtest therefore to have put my money to the exchangers, and then at my coming I should have received mine own with usury. Take therefore the talent from him, and give it unto him which hath ten talents.

For unto every one that hath shall be given, and he shall have abundance: but from him that hath not shall be taken away even that which he hath. And cast ye the unprofitable servant into outer darkness: there shall be weeping and gnashing of teeth.

Stewards Prepare For The Lord's Return

Being a steward to God is the highest honor and privilege in creation. As His steward, you are commissioned with the responsibility to manage and care for all that God gives to you. When He returns, you will give an account for what you have done as a Christian. Are you being a good steward for God?

Have you wondered what God's will is for your life? Have you wondered what you could do to serve Him better? Many Christians wonder how to live for God and what they can do to serve Him. Some feel confused about their role. Others feel like they lack guidance and knowledge of what to do. Most would like to do better, but many do not know what to do with their time, their talents, and their treasures. They have not figured out what to do with what they have.

Aimless Christians wander through life squandering the resources Christ has given them, such as their time, their talents, and their treasures. Carnal Christians gather their possessions for themselves and use their time, talents, and treasures for selfish purposes. Aimless Christians are not close enough to God to know His will, and carnal Christians do not want to love God. The result is the same. Those who do not understand the purpose of their time, talents, and treasures are not good stewards.

Many Christians feel like they are missing something in their walk with the Lord. They feel disappointed in themselves, guilty, and ashamed. They are fearful of making decisions because they do not know how to make good decisions.

This lesson will show you what a good steward is, what a good steward does, and what a good steward can expect from God. Applying the lessons in this study will help you make good decisions, recognize which decisions are good, and anticipate the joy of standing before the Lord Jesus Christ to give Him an account of what you have done for Him.

All Stewards Will Be Held Accountable

First Corinthians 3:11–15 explains that Christians will answer for their stewardship to God.

"For other foundation can no man lay than that is laid, which is Jesus Christ.

Now if any man build upon this foundation gold, silver, precious stones, wood, hay, stubble; Every man's work shall be made manifest: for the day shall declare it, because it shall be revealed by fire; and the fire shall try every man's work of what sort it is.

If any man's work abide which he hath built thereupon, he shall receive a reward. If any man's work shall be burned, he shall suffer loss: but he himself shall be saved; yet so as by fire."

Fortunately, Christians who are bad stewards will still be saved. Christ makes this possible because He builds our foundation. He is our foundation. He makes our foundation perfect and eternal. No one can build a permanent foundation like Him. And nothing can reverse or undo His work.

Nonetheless, all stewards will give an account to God for their stewardship. The works of Christians will be judged. The good works will be rewarded. The bad works will result in loss.

Sadly, the lost will be judged without the foundation of Jesus Christ. All their works will be burned with them in the fires of hell. It is essential that people believe in God's work and promise to save them.

Good Stewards Will Be Rewarded Well

As the parable of the stewards and talents shows, the servants who invested for the Lord received double. That doubling may not occur in this life because this is our investment period. But there are heavenly rewards.

Hebrews 6:10 assures,

"For God is not unrighteous to forget your work and labour of love, which ye have shewed toward his name, in that ye have ministered to the saints, and do minister."

The doubling mentioned in this parable is not about math. It is about being rewarded with more than is invested. Investing your time, talents, and treasures for the Lord guarantees more return.

We Are Stewards Of Our Lord

To be the Lord means to be in charge. Jesus is called the King of kings and Lord of lords. He is the creator of all things. There is none greater than Jesus. He is our Master. He is God. We are His servants.

Jesus asked in Luke 6:46, "And why call ye me, Lord, Lord, and do not the things which I say?"

As our Lord, it is reasonable to listen to Him and *obey* Him. In fact, Jesus is saying that He is Lord to those who obey Him. Is He your Lord? Do you obey Him? Are you doing His will and doing what He expects of you?

Whom do you serve? Who is the Lord of your life?

We Are Stewards Of Our Lord's Possessions

We are entrusted with the Lord's resources. The time, talents, and treasures we have are His resources. Though it is easy to think of these resources as belonging to us, the correct perspective is that everything belongs to God.

First Corinthians 6:19–20 makes clear that even our bodies belong to Him. "What? know ye not that your body is the temple of the Holy Ghost which is in you, which ye have of God, and ye are not your own? For ye are bought with a price: therefore glorify God in your body, and in your spirit, which are God's."

Haggai 2:8 says, "The silver is mine, and the gold is mine, saith the LORD of hosts."

God owns all things and gives all things. We are the stewards of His things.

Our Lord Makes Stewardship Possible And Reasonable

Without Jesus Christ, we were headed toward eternal condemnation. Without Him, there was no hope of eternal joy. Only by His loving grace is our future secured with eternal life and blessings.

Jesus paid for our sins. Due to sin in our lives, we were faced with an impossible payment of an infinite debt. We were faced with having to experience eternal death. We had no hope of ever being able to pay off this infinite debt. Only our eternal God could pay such a debt in full. That is the reason Jesus died.

Romans 5:8 says, "But God commendeth his love toward us, in that, while we were yet sinners, Christ died for us."

John 3:16 says, "For God so loved the world, that he gave his only begotten Son, that whosoever believeth in him should not perish, but have everlasting life."

Jesus sacrificed His life for us to make eternal life possible for us. When we understand what He has done for us, we understand that the only right thing to do is to serve Him.

Romans 12:1 says, "I beseech you therefore, brethren, by the mercies of God, that ye present your bodies a living sacrifice, holy, acceptable unto God, which *is* your reasonable service."

If Jesus was willing to give His life to bless us, does it not seem reasonable to take advantage of His obvious love for us and serve Him? Jesus gave His time, His talents, and His treasures to make our lives possible. What would you like to give Him?

Good Stewards Live For God

In Galatians 2:20, Paul expressed the perspective that he lived for Christ, not for himself. "I am crucified with Christ: nevertheless I live; yet not I, but Christ liveth in me: and the life which I now live in the flesh I live by the faith of the Son of God, who loved me, and gave himself for me."

As stewards of God, we are responsible to do His bidding. He gives us time, talent, and treasures to manage. Everything we do should be for the Lord. First Corinthians 10:31 says, "Whether therefore ye eat, or drink, or whatsoever ye do, do all to the glory of God."

To do anything to the glory of God requires doing what God tells us to do. We must obey Him. We must begin with our love for Him.

Good Stewards Want To Do The Will Of God

Good stewards know that the best path for them is God's will. Nothing else could be better.

God is our Creator and knows what is best for us based on the way He made us. Further, He loves us. He cares about us. He wants only the best for us. He has done everything possible to help us and bless us. For this reason, good stewards seek God's will.

To neglect God's will is to neglect the best path for our lives. To fail in finding and doing God's will is to fail in doing what is best for us.

Good stewards are not afraid to surrender their lives to God. They believe God loves them and cares for them. They know God's will is not to be feared. Rather, they fear not knowing and doing God's

will. They do not want to miss out on the best God has planned
for them.

Have you come to the point in your life of trusting God and
wanting His will for your life? Have you told Him that you want
His will to be done in your life? Have you told Him that, whatever
His will is, you want to experience it?

Good Stewards Love God First

Jesus said in Matthew 22:37–38, "Thou shalt love the Lord thy God
with all thy heart, and with all thy soul, and with all thy mind.
This is the first and great commandment."

Nurturing your love for God is essential as His steward. Loving
God enables you to discern what His will is. If you do not love
Him first and foremost, you will serve yourself. You will not be a
good steward.

Those who love God with all their hearts, souls, and minds will
be good stewards. They will care about the things of God first.
And in doing so, all things will be cared for. Jesus said in Matthew
6:33, "But seek ye first the kingdom of God, and his righteousness,
and all these things shall be added unto you."

Good Stewards Love Others

After telling the lawyer what the first and great command is,
Jesus said in Matthew 22:39, "And the second is like unto it, Thou
shalt love thy neighbour as thyself."

The second priority is to love others as yourself. This is
possible when you love God with all your heart, soul, and
mind.

The most important priority in your life is loving God. The second commandment will follow because God's love in us will produce a love for others.

First John 4:21 says, "And this commandment have we from him, That he who loveth God love his brother also."

Loving others is an indication of your love for God. When you love God, His love controls your life. This in turn will reveal itself as love for others through you. If you do not love God, loving others will not be easy to do.

In John 13:35, Jesus said, "By this shall all men know that ye are my disciples, if ye have love one to another."

When you love God with all your heart, soul, and mind, everything else you do as God's steward will be determined by your love for Him. When you love Him, you will seek His will, listen to His commandments, and obey Him.

For this reason, Jesus said in Matthew 22:40, "On these two commandments hang all the law and the prophets."

Good Stewards Invest In Others

The greatest return in this life is the network of friends you build. This is the example of Jesus. Everything He did was for others.

Jesus healed us. He taught us. He died for us. He guided us. He saved us. And in return, He gained the fellowship of millions of souls.

You can multiply your investment with extreme success by investing your time, talent, and treasures into training others to love the Lord and to serve Him well. The more people you invest in to train them to follow Christ, the more disciples for Christ there will be.

Good stewards understand the mission of their Lord. They understand the desires of their Lord. They understand how to invest in what pleases their Lord the most.

In Luke 19:10, Jesus said, "For the Son of man is come to seek and to save that which was lost."

Jesus came to save souls. His mission was to train others to do likewise. He loves us, and He wants to bless us. He wants us to enjoy fellowship with Him. Because of His love for us, He will do anything to gain our fellowship and to bless us. First John 4:10 says, "Herein is love, not that we loved God, but that he loved us, and sent his Son to be the propitiation for our sins."

A good steward understands the mission of His Lord and will invest his time, talents, and treasures to help fulfill that mission. First John 4:11 says, "Beloved, if God so loved us, we ought also to love one another."

If we love others as God loves us, we will invest all that we have into winning souls to Christ and training them to do likewise. Investing in others is investing for the Lord.

Jesus expressed this sentiment of loving Him by loving others, saying in Matthew 25:34-45,

Then shall the King say unto them on his right hand, Come, ye blessed of my Father, inherit the kingdom prepared for you from the foundation of the world: For I was an hungred, and ye gave me meat: I was thirsty, and ye gave me drink: I was a stranger, and ye took me in: Naked, and ye clothed me: I was sick, and ye visited me: I was in prison, and ye came unto me. Then shall the righteous answer him, saying, Lord, when saw we thee an hungred, and fed thee? or thirsty, and gave thee drink? When saw we thee a stranger, and took thee in? or naked, and clothed thee? Or when saw we thee sick, or in prison, and came unto thee? And the King shall answer and say unto them, Verily I say unto you, Inasmuch as ye have done it unto one of the least of these my brethren, ye have done it unto me. *Then shall he say also unto them on the left hand, Depart from me, ye cursed, into everlasting fire, prepared for the devil and his angels: For I was an hungred, and ye gave me no meat: I was thirsty, and ye gave me no drink: I was a stranger, and ye took me not in: naked, and ye clothed me not: sick, and in prison, and ye visited me not. Then shall they also answer him, saying, Lord, when saw we thee an hungred, or athirst, or a stranger, or naked, or sick, or in prison, and did not minister unto thee? Then shall he answer them, saying, Verily I say unto you, Inasmuch as ye did it not to one of the least of these, ye did it not to me.*

2

GOOD STEWARDS INCREASE THEIR RESOURCES

The better you care for God's resources, the better you care for yourself. Good stewards increase their assets by investing their time, talents, and treasures wisely. The more you gain as a steward, the more you are blessed to invest again and again in the Lord's work. In contrast, when you serve yourself, you will not be a good steward of God's resources, and in the end, you will lose everything.

Good stewards invest their time, talents, and treasures for the Lord to increase His kingdom. This means more souls are saved due to the investment you make to help achieve that goal.

Good stewards invest their assets because they love the Lord and others. We should do everything with and in the love of God. First Corinthians 16:14 reminds us, "Let all your things be done with charity."

Those who love God with all their heart, soul, and mind invest God's resources fully into the mission of God. Good stewards do not hold back. Second Corinthians 9:6–7 says, "But this I say, He which soweth sparingly shall reap also sparingly; and he which soweth bountifully shall reap also bountifully. Every man according as he purposeth in his heart, so let him give; not grudgingly, or of necessity: for God loveth a cheerful giver."

If you want maximum return on your investment for God as a good steward, then invest all your time, talents, and treasures into God's work. Make His mission of winning souls your mission too.

Good Stewards Are Content

In the parable of the talents and stewards, Jesus said that three stewards received different amounts of talents. The Lord knows what we are capable of using and investing. In Philippians 4:11, Paul writes, "Not that I speak in respect of want: for I have learned, in whatsoever state I am, therewith to be content."

Paul's attitude was to be thankful for what God had provided for him. He was content to invest the time, talents, and treasures God had given to him. He certainly had less to work with than many others. He suffered greater obstacles than most. But he invested all that he had, and the return was immense. What can you do for the Lord with the assets He has given you?

Good stewards are not envious of other servants. They are preoccupied with investing the assets the Lord has given to them. They are not fretting over how much more someone else has. Colossians 3:23 admonishes, "And whatsoever ye do, do it heartily, as to the Lord, and not unto men."

Ephesians 6:7 also admonishes, "With good will doing service, as to the Lord, and not to men."

Good stewards pursue investing to increase their assets as much as possible for the Lord. They are concerned about God's mission, not their personal possession.

Further, good stewards understand that encouraging others who serve the Lord is another way to advance the mission of Christ. Encouraging others and building relationships with good stewards is a wonderful way to increase the energy and accomplishments of enlarging the kingdom of God.

Discontentment leads to discouragement and division. It weakens the efforts to advance the cause of Christ. Discontentment means you are focused on yourself and not on God. Let the feeling of discontent or the feeling of envy be reminders to you that you have left your first love and that you need to nurture your love for God. Be thankful to Him for what He has given to you and invest your time, talents, and treasures to His glory.

Learning To Be A Good Steward

Good stewards desire to be better and to do well for God. They are always watching over God's resources and learning ways to improve on the management and investment of their resources. They are diligent students. They learn to correct mistakes, and they learn how to improve.

Learning to be a good steward requires nurturing your love for God. You do this by prayer, by studying His Word, and by learning from the counsel and examples of good stewards in your church.

The Word of God, the Spirit of God, and the church of God are the three vital resources given to us to teach us how to be good stewards. These three resources help us nurture our love for God and provide instruction to help us be better stewards. As you pursue your quest to be the best steward to God you can possibly be, remember to utilize these three resources to the fullest extent.

Good stewards are faithful to God. They are consistent in their habits to learn how to serve God better. By serving Him faithfully, learning is guaranteed. A lot is learned by applying God's counsel and learning from experience.

If you occasionally try to serve God and limit serving Him to what you feel is convenient for you, you will not learn how to be a good steward. For this reason, 1 Corinthians 4:2 says, "Moreover it is required in stewards, that a man be found faithful."

Be consistent and diligent about serving God. If you are, you will be blessed as you serve Him.

God Gives Us Time, Talents, And Treasures

God has given us three resources to invest. He has given us twenty-four hours every day. Every steward receives the same number of hours every day, although some need more sleep than others. We all have the same amount of time, but God has made us different in our sleep requirements.

God has given us talents. As with the differences for sleep, God gives His stewards different talents. Some are artistic, some are mathematicians. Others are artistic mathematicians. Some are capable of hard, manual labor. Some are strong in their organizational skills. Others are great speakers. Some are leaders. Some are followers. Some are brilliant in strategizing ways to succeed in anything they do. Some have magnetic personalities that others are nurtured by. Our talents are gifts from God and skills made possible because of Him.

God also gives us possessions of value. Your treasures are your properties and money. Everything can be converted into treasures of value. Your life, your time, your skills, and your money are all assets given to you by God. If you invest these things wisely, you can increase the value of assets God has given to you.

Good stewards convert their assets of time, talents, and treasures into souls won to Christ. This is the purpose of being given assets as stewards of God. This is God's greatest desire and the desire of every good steward. How well are you converting your time, talents, and treasures into winning souls for Christ?

Different Resources For Different Stewards

In the parable in Matthew 25, God gave the three stewards different talents. The quantity of the talents was not as important as what the stewards did with their talents. The steward with the most invested those talents and gained more. The second steward did not receive as much as the first steward, but he was faithful to invest what he received from the Lord. Regardless of the talents and the amount of talents He gives, God expects His stewards to be faithful to increase those talents.

Squandering Talents Is Wicked

Unprofitable stewards are not faithful to God, do not love God, and do not trust God. They are selfish. They serve themselves. They do not want to invest in the mission of God. They care more about themselves than about souls being condemned for eternity.

Rather than use the time, talents, and treasures God has given for the purpose of winning souls to His kingdom, they squander His assets on pleasing themselves. Using another's possessions for self is theft.

Some stewards try to serve themselves and God. But Jesus said in Matthew 6:24, "No man can serve two masters: for either he will hate the one, and love the other; or else he will hold to the one, and despise the other. Ye cannot serve God and mammon."

To serve mammon means to invest for the purpose of self-gain rather than gain for God. Unprofitable servants do not invest with God's mission in mind. They are thinking only of themselves.

Possessing more talents and treasures does not make a steward unprofitable. Many good stewards have been given great wealth relative to others. Abraham and King Solomon possessed more fame and fortune in their time than others, but they were good stewards. They used their fame and fortune to the glory of God.

However, unprofitable stewards pursue money because they love wealth. Acquiring money for the sake of amassing wealth is their desire. First Timothy 6:10 says, "For the love of money is the root of all evil: which while some coveted after, they have erred from the faith, and pierced themselves through with many sorrows."

Loving money and having money are two different things. The only way to fulfill the first and great commandment is to love God with all your heart, soul, and mind. Those who love money, do not love God. They do not acquire money to invest in God's mission.

In contrast, good stewards who are wealthy, use their assets to further the purpose of Christ. The more they have, the more they invest in God's work.

How Good Stewards Invest Assets For The Lord

Good stewards invest their assets in three ways.

1. For the Lord to His glory.
2. For His mission.
3. With cheerfulness.

Those who love God joyfully give to the cause of Christ to glorify Him. Christ's purpose is their purpose. They want the same thing

Christ wants. Second Corinthians 9:7 says, "Every man according as he purposeth in his heart, so let him give; not grudgingly, or of necessity: for God loveth a cheerful giver."

When God's goal is your goal, you will be very pleased to help fulfill that goal, and you will be pleased when it is fulfilled.

By converting every asset you have into winning souls, you will have more to offer the Lord. He is not interested in time, talent, and treasures. These things are easy to give and take at any time. The destiny of souls, on the other hand, is forever fixed in heaven or hell. God's greatest concern is about winning souls into heaven. This is the greatest concern of good stewards.

What will you give to Christ when you meet Him in heaven? Will you give Him the money He gave you, or will you offer Him the saved souls that came from your investment?

Where Is Your Treasure?

Do you love the Lord more than anything else? A clever way to test yourself is to ask what you would miss the most if you were without it. Another question to ask is what do you work harder for? Your thoughts and your time will be preoccupied with that which is most precious to you. Jesus said in Matthew 6:21, "For where your treasure is, there will your heart be also."

If money is your first love, money will be the thing you miss the most and work hardest for. If you can forget God and not feel a desire to participate in winning and discipling souls, then God is not where your heart is. If you spend more of your time doing things other than advancing the kingdom of God, then God is not where your heart is. If you spend more of your talents on doing things other than advancing the kingdom of God, then God is not where your heart is.

Many Christians neglect thinking seriously about God except for once a year on Easter. Some might think about Him on Sundays because they go to church. Others might think of Him occasionally when it is convenient for them. Despite what we say or know to be right, when we neglect to make God the first concern in our lives every moment of our lives, we are pursuing a greater love and desire.

When we do not have time to serve the Lord, to read our Bible, to participate in church activities, to pray, and to help advance the kingdom of God, we are too busy doing something else more important to us. When we do not have time to devote our talents for ministry because we are using them more on things to make money or to entertain ourselves, then we are not using our talents to the glory of God. When we spend our money on things that please ourselves, to the neglect of advancing the kingdom of God, we are not using our talents to the glory of God.

God wants our heart. He wants us to love Him with all of our heart, soul, and mind. When He has your heart, He will have everything else. He is not asking you to neglect the needs you have in your life. He is asking that He be your most important need.

If you think you do not need God, you have a spiritual problem. If you say you need God, but live like you do not need Him, you have a spiritual problem. If you want to mature spiritually and make the most of your life as a Christian, you need to make God your first love.

3

GOOD STEWARDS MAKE THE BEST USE OF TIME

Do you find that you don't have time for God, for prayer, for church activities, for Bible study, for ministry help? What do you spend your time doing?

The most important thing in your life to pursue is loving God. Jesus said in Matthew 22:37–38, "Thou shalt love the Lord thy God with all thy heart, and with all thy soul, and with all thy mind. This is the first and great commandment."

When your relationship with God is good, and He is your priority, then everything else will fall into place. Everything you do will be for God. Your desire will be to glorify Him and obey Him. You will understand and feel His desires. Those desires will become a part of you. Your purpose in life will become clear, and your priorities will be more certain.

What do your priorities look like? Do you have a list? If so, consider using a circle. Put Christ in the center, and place everything else around the circle. This is a good way to remember that Christ is the reason to do anything. If you have something on your circle that is not for Christ, remove it.

A circle reminds you that there is no arbitrary list of priorities. God is the only priority you should have. He is the one that determines what you should do. There is no second priority to compete with your first priority.

Good Stewards Use Their Time To Do God's Will

Everyone lives with the same amount of daily time. This is one thing that God gives to everyone equally. And yet some are more productive than others.

The difference in productivity can be due to differences in skill. Another reason for differences in productivity may be due to the way productivity is determined. Different jobs produce different results at different rates. The important thing to keep in mind is whether you are using your time for God. Regardless of the results, if you are serving the Lord, you are using your time wisely. Are you using your time wisely?

Colossians 4:5 says, "Walk in wisdom toward them that are without, redeeming the time."

Being exhorted to redeem the time shows us that we need to consider how we use our time. We need to take the issue of managing time seriously. We are admonished to be wise.

For some, productive use of time is a nuisance and unimportant. But good stewards know differently. They redeem their time wisely to advance the kingdom of God and to increase their talents.

Ephesians 5:15–17 says, "See then that ye walk circumspectly, not as fools, but as wise, Redeeming the time, because the days are evil. Wherefore be ye not unwise, but understanding what the will of the Lord is."

The best way to use your time wisely is to do God's will. This requires loving God with all your heart, soul, and mind. This requires serving Him and obeying Him. You may be working hard and staying busy, but are you working wisely? Are you doing His will?

How To Know God's Will

The way to determine the wise use of time is to determine whether you are doing God's will. How do you know God's will?

It is not difficult to determine God's general plan for your life. When you are diligent to study His Word, pray, and participate in His church ministries, you will discover His will. God's will for your life is summed up well by Jesus in John 15:8, "Herein is my Father glorified, that ye bear much fruit; so shall ye be my disciples."

Being a disciple means to follow Christ. Disciples embrace all that is Christ-like. Disciples adopt as their own His lifestyle, His values, His message, and His ambitions.

Because Jesus said His mission was to seek and to save that which was lost (Luke 19:10), your mission in life as His disciple is to seek and to save that which is lost. Because He commands you to be joined to a church, you should do so without hesitation. Because He commissioned His church to go into all nations to make disciples, to establish churches, and to teach His message, you should find some way to participate. Because Christ wants you to be fully matured spiritually and to be in a protective and edifying environment, you should make choices that ensure your participation and membership in His church. Because following Christ leads to ultimate fulfillment, the goals of Christ should serve as the general guidelines for all the decisions you make.

As you study the Word of God and nurture your love for Him, your understanding of God's thoughts will mature. In many cases, you will recognize what Jesus would or would not do even though it is not spelled out in the Bible. The better you know Christ, the better your judgment will be in determining His will.

Good choices are determined by how they contribute to furthering the work of Christ, the saving of souls, the establishing of missions, and the edifying of the saints. Good decisions ensure that your children are raised in a spiritually enriched environment, that you utilize every resource (the Word of God, the Spirit of God, and the church of God), and that you do not jeopardize your spiritual well-being with bad influences.

Overcoming Resistance To Spiritual Growth

Good stewards understand that Christians do not accidently grow. They do not drift aimlessly into maturity. Our natural tendency is to slip into carnality and neglect God's counsel. Wise stewards know they must purposely, with persistence and patience, plan and put effort into growing. We must contend with our flesh, with Satan, with our carnal culture, and with peers who are not interested in serving God.

Paul wrote in 1 Corinthians 9:27, "But I keep under my body, and bring it into subjection: lest that by any means, when I have preached to others, I myself should be a castaway."

Ephesians 6:12 reminds us, "We wrestle not against flesh and blood, but against principalities, against powers, against the rulers of the darkness of this world, against spiritual wickedness in high places."

Jude 1:3 admonishes, "Beloved, when I gave all diligence to write unto you of the common salvation, it was needful for me to write unto you, and exhort you that ye should earnestly contend for the faith which was once delivered unto the saints."

First Corinthians 3:3 says, "For ye are yet carnal: for whereas there is among you envying, and strife, and divisions, are ye not carnal, and walk as men?"

Our walk with Christ is always being challenged and is always fraught with obstacles. But good stewards know the promise in Philippians 4:13 for guaranteed success to mature spiritually. "I can do all things through Christ which strengtheneth me."

Striving with diligence to fight the good fight, to contend with falsehoods and false teachers, to resist the natural tendencies in our flesh, and to bring our bodies under subjection requires first of all yielding to God. By yielding to God, we experience His strength and wisdom to overcome anything that would cause us to stumble in our walk with Christ. Yielding comes with making God our first love above all other things.

Setting Goals For Good Stewardship

Without goals we will not grow like we should. Goals give direction, measurement for learning, and accountability.

Goals Are Biblical.

There are many personal goals recorded in the Bible. Here a few:

1. God gave Noah the goal of building an ark.

2. God gave Joshua the goal of taking the Israelites to the promised land.

3. David had a goal to destroy Goliath.

4. Solomon had a goal to build the temple for God.

5. Abraham had a goal of finding a wife for his son.

6. Jesus Christ had a goal to die for our sins.

7. Jesus has a goal to seek and to save those who are lost.

Were these goals fulfilled? We see that they were. In each case, these goals were specific and clear. They gave direction, and others could determine whether they were fulfilled or not.

Goals are Biblical, and God has specific goals for our lives. We will know these goals when God is our priority. We will know them from His Word, through prayer, and by counseling with leaders in our churches.

Goals Are Important.

1. Goals give direction to our lives. It is impossible for a person to press toward a mark if there is no mark.
2. Goals ensure progress. The accomplishment of goals will show progress in our lives.
3. Goals get us out of confusion and aimlessness. They help us to understand and to remember what needs to be done and why.
4. Goals help us stay focused on future possibilities rather than on failures.
5. Goals help us to sort out the demands on our time. If we know what we intend to do, then it is much easier for us to recognize when our time is being wasted or used improperly.

Goals Based On Priorities.

Our goals should be based on what is most important to God and on His will for us. We are His servants. We should be seeking to do His will and to fulfill His goals. What is important to God?

First, He wants us to love Him. Our fellowship is top priority with God. Second, He wants us to help others love Him. This involves winning souls to Christ by sharing the Gospel and by training disciples to do likewise.

You should think of yourself as a disciple who is a student, or a disciple who is a carpenter, or a disciple who is a business owner, or a disciple who is a homemaker, or a disciple who is an employee. Your identity should be a disciple of Jesus Christ. Following Christ is the most important thing that you will ever do. How will you use your career or skills to serve the Lord?

We know from the Scriptures that God commands us to be disciples, witness to others about our faith, participate in a local church, study His Word, and pray. These are basic activities that should be in every Christian's list of things to do. Your status as a student, employee, or business owner is a platform for your ministry.

As disciples, we should make God's priorities our priorities. Then we fit everything else into our schedule of ministry. If we reverse our priorities and pursue our education or career first, then we will not have time for God or His priorities.

Can you share the Gospel message and lead someone to the Lord? Can you show others how to study the Bible? Do you participate in your church ministries to make them better? Do you encourage others to thrive in their personal ministries of discipleship?

Goals That Are Important.

Don't let circumstances control you. Control your circumstances. Determine how you can best serve God and contribute to His cause and then do it. Good stewards don't waste their time, talents, or treasures. Each resource is precious, whether it is time, money, or skills.

Steps to Reach Your Goals.

1. Ask God what goals you should pursue. God will help you pursue the goals He gives you.
2. Have a clear picture of your goals. You should be able to tell others what your goals are. If you are struggling to describe your goals, you are struggling to fulfill your goals.
3. Have confidence that you can fulfill your goals. If God has set your goals, then nothing can prevent you from fulfilling them. Paul said in Philippians 4:13, "I can do all things through Christ which strengtheneth me." First Thessalonians 5:24 says, "Faithful is he that calleth you, who also will do it."
4. Do it.

Profile Of A Disciple

The following chart is an example of goals to pursue in doctrine, character, and skills. Are there any areas you need to work on to improve your personal ministry?

Profile of a Disciple

*Spiritual Birthday:*_____   *Baptism date:*_____

Character_____

Abiding in Christ	Faithful	Obedient
Anticipating Christ's	Forgiving	Optimistic
return	Generous	Patient
Application of the Word	Good hygiene	Problem solver
Assured of salvation	Good witness	Punctual
Biblical priorities	Gracious	Reliable
Cares about others	Happy	Responsible
Christian fellowship	Helpful	Sacrificial
Church home	Humble	Separation from sin
Close to God	Kind	Servant heart
Consistent prayer	Know God's will	Supportive
Dependable	Loving	Teachable
Desires to mature	Modest appearance	Thankful
Edifying speech	Modest relationships	Victory over sin
Encouraging	Modest speech	Vigilant to Satan's devices

Ministry Skills_____

Bible reading program	Follow-up	Share testimony
Bible study and lesson	Meet new people	Time management
development	Memorization	Use talents
Build friendships	Prayer	Witnessing
Daily devotion	Prayer journal	
Financial stewardship	Share Gospel	

Doctrine_____

Angels	Heaven	Sanctification
Bible	Holy Spirit	Satan
Bible survey	Jesus Christ	Sin
Church	Leadership	Spiritual Growth
Discipleship	Missions	Tongues/Charismatics
God	Salvation	

Evaluating How You Spend Your Time

How much time do you spend serving the Lord? It should be 100 percent of the time. Everything you do should be for the Lord.

Do you struggle with finding time to do the essential things God has asked you to do? A good way to evaluate how you spend your time and to determine how to use your time better is to use a time budget chart.

The time budget chart below is an example. Change the time interval to one that works best for you.

Time Chart

	Sunday	Monday	Tuesday	Wednesday	Thursday	Friday	Saturday
6:00 am							
7:00am							
8:00am							
9:00 am							
10:00 am							
11:00 am							
12:00 pm							
1:00 pm							
2:00 pm							
3:00 pm							
4:00 pm							
5:00 pm							
6:00 pm							
7:00 pm							
8:00 pm							
9:00 pm							
10:00 pm							

God never asks you to do too much. If you feel there is too much to do, either you are doing more than He has asked you to do, or you are not using your time wisely.

Making Good Use Of Time By Delegating

Leaders are assigned goals that are beyond what they have time to do personally. For example, Moses provided counsel to the children of God but was overwhelmed by the number of people wanting to talk to him. His time was spent counseling from morning to evening. There was no time left to do anything else.

Exodus 18:13–24 records the challenge Moses faced and the advice his father-in-law, the priest of Midian, gave him. Verse 13 says, "And it came to pass on the morrow, that Moses sat to judge the people: and the people stood by Moses from the morning unto the evening."

Verses 17–18 say, "Moses' father in law said unto him, The thing that thou doest is not good. Thou wilt surely wear away, both thou, and this people that is with thee: for this thing is too heavy for thee; thou art not able to perform it thyself alone."

In verses 21–22, Jethro recommends delegating responsibilities. "Moreover, thou shalt provide out of all the people able men, such as fear God, men of truth, hating covetousness; and place such over them, to be rulers of thousands, and rulers of hundreds, rulers of fifties, and rulers of tens: And let them judge the people at all seasons: and it shall be, that every great matter they shall bring unto thee, but every small matter they shall judge: so shall it be easier for thyself, and they shall bear the burden with thee."

In verse 23, Jethro advises Moses to seek God's guidance and confirmation that He approved of Jethro's advice. "If thou shalt do this thing, and God command thee so, then thou shalt be able to endure, and all this people shall also go to their place in peace."

Verse 24 says, "So Moses hearkened to the voice of his father in law, and did all that he had said."

By delegating responsibilities, bigger goals can be fulfilled.

Making Good Use Of Time With Efficiency

Two people given the same task often need different amounts of time to complete the task. Some can get a lot more done each day than others because they have learned how to be efficient with their time.

Anyone can improve the efficiency of their time with a little thoughtfulness and effort. Using your time efficiently requires being intentional about trying to do more with the time you have.

Consider applying the following tips to make better use of your time.

1. Get sufficient rest.
2. Stay healthy.
3. Resolve conflicts that drain you emotionally and preoccupy your thoughts.
4. Designate time to work undisturbed.
5. Rest your brain with short breaks.
6. Organize your projects with checklists to stay on task.
7. Write down brilliant ideas to look at later to avoid being distracted and forgetting.
8. Plan tasks to do for the next day.

4

GOOD STEWARDS IMPROVE AND USE THEIR TALENTS

Every person has abilities that make certain tasks easy to do and preferred. These abilities are also called talents, skills, and gifts.

A talented person is one who does something very well. It may be a natural talent, or it may be a developed skill resulting from hours of practice. If the talent is supernaturally granted from God, it is called a gift.

The words talent, skill, and gift are difficult to distinguish because they are used interchangeably and inconsistently. The important thing to understand about talents is that all aptitudes come from God and should be used to serve God. James 1:17 says, "Every good gift and every perfect gift is from above, and cometh down from the Father of lights, with whom is no variableness, neither shadow of turning."

People do what comes easily or is convenient for them. For this reason, the aptitudes are always manifested. Aptitudes are a part of who we are. They define who we are. They are easily seen in us. Aptitudes are not hidden qualities we need to search for.

If you are musically inclined, you probably play an instrument. If you are verbally inclined, you probably write. If you like to organize things, you may be an administrator.

Good stewards use their talents to serve the Lord. Craftsmen make things for their church. Administrators organize and manage things done in the church. Musicians play for the Lord. Any skills you use for your employer or for yourself are skills you should be using for the Lord.

Gifts from God should be used for God. Colossians 3:17 says, "And whatsoever ye do in word or deed, do all in the name of the Lord Jesus, giving thanks to God and the Father by him."

First Corinthians 12:4–11 explains how the Spirit gives different gifts to accomplish His will. "Now there are diversities of gifts, but the same Spirit. And there are differences of administrations, but the same Lord. And there are diversities of operations, but it is the same God which worketh all in all. But the manifestation of the Spirit is given to every man to profit withal. For to one is given by the Spirit the word of wisdom; to another the word of knowledge by the same Spirit; To another faith by the same Spirit; to another the gifts of healing by the same Spirit; To another the working of miracles; to another prophecy; to another discerning of spirits; to another divers kinds of tongues; to another the interpretation of tongues: But all these worketh that one and the selfsame Spirit, dividing to every man severally as he will."

First Peter 4:10–11 says everything should be done to glorify the Lord. "As every man hath received the gift, even so minister the same one to another, as good stewards of the manifold grace of God. If any man speak, let him speak as the oracles of God; if any man minister, let him do it as of the ability which God giveth: that God in all things may be glorified through Jesus Christ, to whom be praise and dominion for ever and ever. Amen." Good stewards use their talents to glorify God, to build up His ministry, and to help their churches thrive.

Stewards Are Blessed With Wisdom For Their Skill

When God gives us a gift, it comes with wisdom to do it. This know-how is granted from God. When there is something to do, God will grant the wisdom to know how to do it.

Exodus 28:3, "And thou shalt speak unto all that are wise hearted, whom I have filled with the spirit of wisdom, that they may make Aaron's garments to consecrate him, that he may minister unto me in the priest's office."

Exodus 36:1, "Then wrought Bezaleel and Aholiab, and every wise hearted man, in whom the LORD put wisdom and understanding to know how to work all manner of work for the service of the sanctuary, according to all that the LORD had commanded."

Exodus 35:25–26, "And all the women that were wise hearted did spin with their hands, and brought that which they had spun, both of blue, and of purple, and of scarlet, and of fine linen. And all the women whose heart stirred them up in wisdom spun goats' hair."

Isaiah 61:1, "The Spirit of the Lord GOD is upon me; because the LORD hath anointed me to preach good tidings unto the meek; he hath sent me to bind up the brokenhearted, to proclaim liberty to the captives, and the opening of the prison to them that are bound."

When God raised up Daniel, Shadrach, Meshach, and Abednego to minister in the king's court of Babylon, God provided them with knowledge and skill. Daniel 1:17 says, "As for these four children, God gave them knowledge and skill in all learning and wisdom: and Daniel had understanding in all visions and dreams."

Spiritual gifts provide talents that congregations need in order to enhance their ministry. Collectively, the different gifts are useful to accomplish the same goal of winning souls and training disciples for Christ.

Discerning Your Gift From God

Talent is easily recognized because talent is the ability to do something well. Ask yourself what you enjoy doing, what you understand well, and what you do well.

You may know what your gifts are because you recognize your talent. Are you using your talent to do God's will? If you are good at doing something, you should be doing it to fulfill the work of winning souls and training disciples. If you are a carpenter, you should be using your skill to build and maintain the church facilities. If you are a teacher, you should be using your skill to teach the Word of God. If you are an accountant, you should be using your skill to help your church with bookkeeping.

God gifts you with talent to fulfill His will for your life. If you are struggling to determine your gift, you need to put effort into discerning God's will for your life. God's will for your life will be supplied with the gifts you need to fulfill His will. If you do not know what your gifts are, you do not know God's will.

The lists of gifts in the Bible are not exhaustive. They are examples. There are many gifts that God gives. Gifts are given to fulfill His will for your life and for your church.

Paul named some offices that benefit the church in Ephesians 4:11–12, which says, "And he gave some, apostles; and some, prophets; and some, evangelists; and some, pastors and teachers;

For the perfecting of the saints, for the work of the ministry, for the edifying of the body of Christ."

In Romans 12:6–8, Paul wrote of personal gifts: "Having then gifts differing according to the grace that is given to us, whether prophecy, let us prophesy according to the proportion of faith; Or ministry, let us wait on our ministering: or he that teacheth, on teaching; Or he that exhorteth, on exhortation: he that giveth, let him do it with simplicity; he that ruleth, with diligence; he that sheweth mercy, with cheerfulness."

Regardless of the role, the responsibility, or God's will, God will provide the skill and wisdom you need to fulfill His will. The important thing to keep in mind is that gifts are given to fulfill God's will, not your will.

When people focus on talents, they often overlook the purpose of gifts. For this reason, it is important to stay focused on God. Gifts are obvious when we know God's will for our lives.

In 1 Corinthians 12:29–31, Paul wrote, "Are all apostles? are all prophets? are all teachers? are all workers of miracles? Have all the gifts of healing? do all speak with tongues? do all interpret? But covet earnestly the best gifts: and yet shew I unto you a more excellent way." People who focus on gifts lose sight of the most important things.

Paul explained in 1 Corinthians 13:1–3 that the thing more important than any gift is love. "Though I speak with the tongues of men and of angels, and have not charity, I am become as sounding brass, or a tinkling cymbal. And though I have the gift of prophecy, and understand all mysteries, and all knowledge; and though I have all faith, so that I could remove mountains, and have not charity, I am nothing. And though I bestow all my goods to feed the poor, and though I give my body to be burned, and have not charity, it profiteth me nothing."

Good stewards nurture their love for God. This leads to knowing God's will. The gifts they receive to fulfill God's will are the result of pursuing the most important things. Good stewards know their gifts because they seek the Lord, not their gifts.

The Desire Of Good Stewards

Good stewards use their talents for God's glory. This means they use their skills to help win souls and train disciples. This is the priority. This is God's will, and they do it willingly because they love Him.

Exodus 35:21 and 29 explain how the children of Israel contributed to the building of the tabernacle. "And they came, every one whose heart stirred him up, and every one whom his spirit made willing, and they brought the LORD'S offering to the work of the tabernacle of the congregation, and for all his service, and for the holy garments.... The children of Israel brought a willing offering unto the LORD, every man and woman, whose heart made them willing to bring for all manner of work, which the LORD had commanded to be made by the hand of Moses."

Good stewards rejoice and willingly give their time, talent, and treasures to the Lord's work because they have been redeemed and saved by God. They love him. First Chronicles 29:9 says, "Then the people rejoiced, for that they offered willingly, because with perfect heart they offered willingly to the LORD: and David the king also rejoiced with great joy." They had a perfect heart because they were saved, and they were nurturing their love for God.

Due to having perfect hearts for God, good stewards feel eager to serve the Lord. It pleases them. They are energized and zealous to work for the Lord.

Those who struggle with serving the Lord and with using their talents for God's work hinder the Lord's purpose. Their gifts are not contributing to the Lord's work. They have time to work for their employer and for themselves, but not for the Lord. If all Christians were willing to use their talents for the Lord, more churches would be flourishing, more souls would hear the Gospel, and more disciples would be trained. These stewards will give an account to God for their lack of willingness to serve God with the talents given to them.

Gifts Are For God, Not For Contest

Talents, skills, and gifts are blessings from God to further His work. Stewards receive different gifts because of the needs in God's work. One person cannot do all things just as one organ in your body cannot do all things. Your eye cannot hear, and your foot cannot pump blood. God gives His stewards different roles and expects everyone to work together.

First Corinthians 12:14–18 says, "For the body is not one member, but many. If the foot shall say, Because I am not the hand, I am not of the body; is it therefore not of the body? And if the ear shall say, Because I am not the eye, I am not of the body; is it therefore not of the body? If the whole body were an eye, where were the hearing? If the whole were hearing, where were the smelling? But now hath God set the members every one of them in the body, as it hath pleased him."

Gifts are not given as rewards to identify who is better than another. They are not given to use as weapons or as indicators of spirituality. They are not to be used to compare or to engage in contest. They are given to accomplish God's work. He expects us to use our gifts as a team and to work together.

Gifts are from God. They are not achievements. We do not possess gifts for our own glory. We should always be thankful to God for our gifts. First Corinthians 4:7 says, "For who maketh thee to differ from another? and what hast thou that thou didst not receive? now if thou didst receive it, why dost thou glory, as if thou hadst not received it?"

GOOD STEWARDS USE THEIR TREASURES FOR GOD'S WORK

Good stewards use their money to advance the cause of Christ. Their desire is to see souls won and disciples trained. For this reason, they fully manage their money to meet the funding needs of the Lord's ministries. They know how to convert money and assets into ministry efforts that save souls.

Are Money And Wealth Evil?

Job, Abraham, Isaac, Jacob, David, and Solomon are a few examples of wealthy saints. Their wealth was a blessing from God. They gave God credit for their wealth. Obviously, money and wealth are not evil.

Nonetheless, being wealthy can lead to problems. First Timothy 6:17–19 says, "Charge them that are rich in this world, that they be not high-minded, nor trust in uncertain riches, but in the living God, who giveth us richly all things to enjoy; That they do good, that they be rich in good works, ready to distribute, willing to communicate; Laying up in store for themselves a good foundation against the time to come, that they may lay hold on eternal life."

Wealth can cause people to be proud. They may look down on people due to differences in wealth. They may depend on their wealth and abilities rather than depend on God. Psalm 62:10 cautions, "If riches increase, set not your heart upon them." Good stewards use their wealth to advance the Lord's work and are thankful to God for their blessings.

Money can be used for evil purposes. Some use money for acquiring power, manipulating people, enslaving others, purchasing drugs, doing illegal things, and indulging their carnal desires. The evil in these cases is in the people using the money.

The Bible does not explain the point at which a person is wealthy. Some think they are wealthy because they have more than others. The sins associated with money are not in how much one has but in how they think about money and use it. For this reason, the warnings that come with wealth can occur at any level of wealth.

Money is not evil. It is a resource for putting food on the table, for staying warm in the winter, for staying cool in the summer, and for funding the Lord's ministries.

Good stewards keep in mind that their wealth is a blessing from God that can easily be lost due to poor investment decisions, poor judgment in managing money, or loss of health. For this reason, they are grateful to God for their wealth, and they seek ways to serve God with their wealth.

The Love Of Money Is Sin

First Timothy 6:9–10 says, "But they that will be rich fall into temptation and a snare, and into many foolish and hurtful lusts, which drown men in destruction and perdition. For the love of money is the root of all evil: which while some coveted after, they have erred from the faith, and pierced themselves through with many sorrows."

Pursuing money rather than God leads people away from God. They lose rewards in heaven, and they fail to use their money for the Lord's work. They are wayward servants who serve themselves rather than God.

Regardless of the amount of money they have, people who love money will always want more. Ecclesiastes 5:10 cautions, "He that loveth silver shall not be satisfied with silver; nor he that loveth abundance with increase: this is also vanity." The love for money will create a need that is never satisfied.

Proverbs 23:4–5 advises, "Labour not to be rich: cease from thine own wisdom. Wilt thou set thine eyes upon that which is not? for riches certainly make themselves wings; they fly away as an eagle toward heaven." Money is temporary and is always subject to being lost. God, on the other hand, is everlasting and will always be with you.

Good stewards love the Lord, not their money. They view their money as a resource provided by the Lord to use for His purposes.

How Is The Love Of Money A Spiritual Problem?

In Mark 4:18–19, Jesus explained the reason some do not get saved or fail to mature spiritually. "And these are they which are sown among thorns; such as hear the word, And the cares of this world, and the deceitfulness of riches, and the lusts of other things entering in, choke the word, and it becometh unfruitful." Money loved is money worshiped. Those who love money will make decisions based on acquiring more money rather than on loving the Lord and winning more souls to Christ. They will neglect God's work for their own work.

In Matthew 22:36–40, Jesus said the first and great commandment is to love God. The love of anything more than God is evil. For this reason, the love of money is sin. Money should not be your first love. You should not pursue money more than the salvation of souls. Time, thoughts, and efforts should be spent for the purpose of winning souls and making disciples. Money should be viewed as a resource to accomplish the Lord's goals.

Working for money to provide for your needs, the needs of your family, the needs of your church, and the needs of ministries is necessary. Believers are admonished to be responsible. Good stewards are responsible, and they pursue fulfilling their obligations. But when the pursuit is to fulfill the lust for money, then there is a problem.

The love for money is the desire to make more money for the sake of having more money to the neglect of God's ministry. Matthew 6:19–21 says, "Lay not up for yourselves treasures upon earth, where moth and rust doth corrupt, and where thieves break through and steal: But lay up for yourselves treasures in heaven, where neither moth nor rust doth corrupt, and where thieves do not break through nor steal: For where your treasure is, there will your heart be also."

When you love money more than God, you may try to pursue both. But your devotion will be divided between the two. You will have to make a choice. Matthew 6:24 says, "No man can serve two masters: for either he will hate the one, and love the other; or else he will hold to the one, and despise the other. Ye cannot serve God and mammon."

The choice to pursue God or to pursue wealth is a choice between God's goals and your goals, God's will and your will.

Good stewards know that God is where security and blessings are. His will is the only safe path to travel. Proverbs 11:28 says, "He that trusteth in his riches shall fall: but the righteous shall flourish as a branch."

The Wealthy Can Be Good Stewards Too

In Matthew 19:16–24, a young man came to Jesus and asked, "Good Master, what good thing shall I do, that I may have eternal life? And he said unto him, Why callest thou me good? there is none good but one, that is, God: but if thou wilt enter into life, keep the commandments. He saith unto him, Which? Jesus said, Thou shalt do no murder, Thou shalt not commit adultery, Thou shalt not steal, Thou shalt not bear false witness, Honour thy father and thy mother: and, Thou shalt love thy neighbour as thyself. The young man saith unto him, All these things have I kept from my youth up: what lack I yet? Jesus said unto him, If thou wilt be perfect, go and sell that thou hast, and give to the poor, and thou shalt have treasure in heaven: and come and follow me. But when the young man heard that saying, he went away sorrowful: for he had great possessions. Then said Jesus unto his disciples, Verily I say unto you, That a rich man shall hardly enter into the kingdom of heaven. And again I say unto you, It is easier for a camel to go through the eye of a needle, than for a rich man to enter into the kingdom of God."

In this passage, Jesus told His disciples that a rich man will not enter heaven. How can that be? Can't wealthy people be saved and be good stewards? It depends on how they view their possessions.

Like the rich young man in Matthew 19, many people are fearful of serving Christ and of pursuing His will for their lives because they do not want to give up their possessions. Christ is not first in their lives, and they do not want Him to be first. Their goal is to be wealthy and comfortable. They are not willing to risk losing opportunities for wealth to follow Christ.

Unlike the rich young man, good stewards have the attitude that they do not possess money and that they are not possessed by money. Rather, they see themselves as managers of *God's* money for His glory. Therefore, good stewards do not consider themselves to be rich. On the other hand, many good stewards are wealthy. They thrive to the glory of God and fulfill His goals because they make good decisions about increasing wealth to God's glory.

God does not require everyone to live in poverty. His will is to bless us, not to curse us. But God's blessings are not determined by how much money we have but by our experience of loving Him regardless of our circumstances.

Ironically, Jesus gave up all He had to make heavenly wealth possible. In 2 Corinthians 8:9, Paul wrote, "For ye know the grace of our Lord Jesus Christ, that, though he was rich, yet for your sakes he became poor, that ye through his poverty might be rich."

What Is The Biblical Perspective On Wealth?

Jesus promises those who believe in Him, "In my Father's house are many mansions: if it were not so, I would have told you. I go to prepare a place for you" (John 14:2). Revelation 21:21 says of the heavenly city, "And the twelve gates were twelve pearls; every several gate was of one pearl: and the street of the city was pure gold, as it were transparent glass."

God is not opposed to wealth. There are examples in the Bible of very wealthy men of God. Many believers are wealthy compared to others. And He wants us to anticipate the riches in heaven. But those riches are in the context of following Christ into heaven. It is by His will and no other.

Wealth is from God. Deuteronomy 8:17–18 says, "And thou say in thine heart, My power and the might of mine hand hath gotten me this wealth. thou shalt remember the LORD thy God: for it is he that giveth thee power to get wealth, that he may establish his covenant which he sware unto thy fathers, as it is this day."

God does not consider poverty and being needy a good thing. Proverbs 13:18 says, "Poverty and shame shall be to him that refuseth instruction: but he that regardeth reproof shall be honoured."

Good stewards have something to give. Paul said in Acts 20:35, "I have shewed you all things, how that so labouring ye ought to support the weak, and to remember the words of the Lord Jesus, how he said, It is more blessed to give than to receive." If you have very little to take care of yourself, you have little, if anything, to help others with. You become dependent on others to help you take care of yourself.

Living in a world of sin and Satan, people are going to suffer deprivation, poverty, and dependence. Jesus said in Mark 14:7, "For ye have the poor with you always, and whensoever ye will ye may do them good: but me ye have not always." Being poor is not always due to a fault of their own. Illness and accidents can prevent people from being wise and vital enough to manage their assets.

The problem with wealth is the temptation of pride and self-sufficiency. The Bible warns the wealthy to beware of these dangers. Thus, believers are exhorted to be content and to seek God's love rather than the world's riches.

Proverbs 30:8–9 says, "Remove far from me vanity and lies: give me neither poverty nor riches; feed me with food convenient for me: Lest I be full, and deny thee, and say, Who is the LORD? or lest I be poor, and steal, and take the name of my God in vain."

Good stewards are concerned about their relationship with the Lord. They stay alert to the danger of not being content and not being thankful. They pray and nurture their relationship with God to avoid being tempted by abundance or by unmet needs. They desire to be blessed with having enough to meet all their needs, and they desire to have money to help finance ministries.

Hebrews 13:5 admonishes us to be content. "Let your conversation be without covetousness; and be content with such things as ye have: for he hath said, I will never leave thee, nor forsake thee." If, through managing the wealth God gives you, your assets increase, praise God for the blessing and be content. If your assets do not increase, despite your efforts, praise God for what you have and be content.

The more assets you have, the more you have to invest in the Lord's work. The less you have, the less you have to invest in the Lord's work. Second Corinthians 9:6–8 says, "But this I say, He which soweth sparingly shall reap also sparingly; and he which soweth bountifully shall reap also bountifully. Every man according as he purposeth in his heart, so let him give; not grudgingly, or of necessity: for God loveth a cheerful giver. And God is able to make all grace abound toward you; that ye, always having all sufficiency in all things, may abound to every good work."

As the parable of the talents shows, God does not give everyone the same amount of talents to invest. But regardless of the amount, be content with whatever God has given you to manage, and invest it to increase those assets to God's glory.

Is it possible to have too much money? There is no limit to how much money God can give to His stewards. He gives different stewards differing amounts of money to manage. Stewards should resist the temptation to compare themselves with others, to be covetous, and to look down on others who have less. Good stewards are content and thankful for what God gives them, and they strive to use their assets to His glory.

How much money does a good steward give to God? Good stewards do not possess their assets. They manage the assets given to them by God. All their assets belong to God. They give everything to God. As managers of assets, stewards find ways to sustain revenue and increase their investments in the Lord's work.

Essentials For Good Stewardship Of Wealth

Health, wisdom, and diligence are essential to good stewardship of assets. Without mental health, there is no ability to think well. Without physical health, there is limited ability to work. Without wisdom, there is no ability to make good decisions to invest for good returns. Without diligence, there is a lack of effort to do what is desired.

Good stewards understand that converting health into wealth is essential and temporary. People struggling with health issues, whether due to neglect of hygiene, nutrition and exercise, or due to disease and accidents, are hindered in being able to work hard and undistracted. A lack of health results in slow thinking, slow work, and lower productivity. For this reason, good stewards plan for their decline in health.

Wisdom is essential for making good decisions about how to manage the assets God gives to you. Good stewards know that, because assets are from God, then His wisdom is needed to make good choices. Wise stewards know their relationship with God is vital to discerning His will and making good decisions. They know they must pray for His guidance when they make decisions.

Wise stewards diligently pursue investing their assets to increase the work of the Lord. They know that the desire to serve God is different from serving God. Stewards who succeed at investing their assets have been diligent at doing the work required to invest. Lazy and irresponsible people are poor stewards. They invest little effort and receive little in return.

Money is the reward of wisdom, good health, and diligent effort. Health and wisdom come from God. Diligence is the effort you put into using the wisdom and health God gives to you.

The Ministry Of Tithing

In the parable of servants and talents, Jesus indicates that He expects His servants to invest and increase their talents and treasures. Those who do are good stewards. And they will convert their increase into winning souls for the Lord. The goal is to increase the number of souls saved by whatever means the Lord gives you and in whatever ways He directs you.

As mentioned before, all that we have belongs to the Lord. Everything we are stewards of should be used to fulfill God's purpose. One of the ways God expects us to invest is to give a tenth of our earnings to His church. The Old Testament Law required Israel to give a tithe of all their increase, and the New Testament teaches tithing as well.

Deuteronomy 14:22 says, "Thou shalt truly tithe all the increase of thy seed, that the field bringeth forth year by year." Leviticus 27:30 says, "And all the tithe of the land, whether of the seed of the land, or of the fruit of the tree, is the LORD'S: it is holy unto the LORD." And Leviticus 27:32 says, "And concerning the tithe of the herd, or of the flock, even of whatsoever passeth under the rod, the tenth shall be holy unto the LORD."

The tithe was given to the priests to be used for the Lord's work. Nehemiah 10:38 says, "And the priest the son of Aaron shall be with the Levites, when the Levites take tithes: and the Levites shall bring up the tithe of the tithes unto the house of our God, to the chambers, into the treasure house."

One tenth of one's increase was designated exclusively for the Lord's priests to use for His work, and the remaining ninety percent was used to increase the Lord's work through His stewards. The priests used the tithe to increase the spirituality of Israel, and the remaining ninety percent was used by individuals to choose how they would serve the Lord.

The tithe continues under the New Testament. There are men of God who minister of the holy things, and, in most cases, there are church facilities to care for. Paul wrote in 1 Corinthians 9:13–14, "Do ye not know that they which minister about holy things live of the things of the temple? and they which wait at the altar are partakers with the altar? Even so hath the Lord ordained that they which preach the gospel should live of the gospel." Christians should be giving a tithe of their increase to their churches.

Some think that giving tithes was exclusive to Israel under the Old Testament. But Paul explains in Hebrews 7 that this is not the case. He refers to the example of Abraham, who gave a tithe to the priest Melchisedec. Abraham did this before the Old Testament law was given. And Jesus' priesthood today is after the order of Melchisedec.

In Hebrews 7:1-2, Paul writes, "For this Melchisedec, king of Salem, priest of the most high God, who met Abraham returning from the slaughter of the kings, and blessed him; To whom also Abraham gave a tenth part of all...." He continues in verse 4, "Now consider how great this man was, unto whom even the patriarch Abraham gave the tenth of the spoils."

Melchisedec was a priest before Levi and Moses were born. This was before the nation of Israel and before the Old Testament

Law. In other words, before the tithe was encoded into law for Israel, tithing was already being practiced. It was something people did without instruction from the Law.

Paul further explains that offering a tithe to the priest Melchisedec was better than the tithes offered under the Old Testament. Hebrews 7:5-7 says, "And verily they that are of the sons of Levi, who receive the office of the priesthood, have a commandment to take tithes of the people according to the law, that is, of their brethren, though they come out of the loins of Abraham: But he whose descent is not counted from them received tithes of Abraham, and blessed him that had the promises. And without all contradiction the less is blessed of the better." In other words, Abraham, from whom the priests of Levi descend, paid tithes to someone not related to him, Israel, or Moses. And Paul states this makes the priesthood of Melchisedec better. Paul goes further to emphasize how much greater Melchisedec the priest is than Abraham and Levi, saying in verses 8-10 that the Levitical priests who received tithes were paying tithes to Melchisedec through Abraham.

Paul goes even further with the superiority of Melchisedec's priesthood, saying in verses 11-16, "If therefore perfection were by the Levitical priesthood, (for under it the people received the law,) what further need was there that another priest should rise after the order of Melchisedec, and not be called after the order of Aaron? For the priesthood being changed, there is made of necessity a change also of the law. For he of whom these things are spoken pertaineth to another tribe, of which no man gave attendance at the altar. For it is evident that our Lord sprang out of Juda; of which tribe Moses spake nothing concerning priesthood. And it is yet far more evident: for that after the similitude of Melchisedec there ariseth another priest, Who is made, not after the law of a carnal commandment, but after the power of an endless life."

The significance of Melchisedec's priesthood being better than Levi's under the Old Testament is how we should be thinking about Jesus. Jesus is a priest after the order of Melchisedec, not after the order of Levi under the Old Covenant. Paul wrote in Hebrews 7:17, "For he testifieth, Thou art a priest for ever after the order of Melchisedec." And in verse 21, he writes, "For those priests were made without an oath; but this with an oath by him that said unto him, The Lord sware and will not repent, Thou art a priest for ever after the order of Melchisedec."

The point is that if Abraham gave tithes to the priest Melchisedec, then we should do likewise. We should give tithes of our increase to the church of our high priest, Jesus Christ, who is our priest after the order of Melchisedec.

The Ministry Of Giving

Mark 12:41–44 says, "And Jesus sat over against the treasury, and beheld how the people cast money into the treasury: and many that were rich cast in much. And there came a certain poor widow, and she threw in two mites, which make a farthing. And he called unto him his disciples, and saith unto them, Verily I say unto you, That this poor widow hath cast more in, than all they which have cast into the treasury: For all they did cast in of their abundance; but she of her want did cast in all that she had, even all her living."

During the days of Jesus, the tithes were given to the treasury of the temple. Jesus observed how a tithe from well-to-do worshippers did not impact their personal living choices. But for the poor widow, the tithe meant she was sacrificing some portion of necessities for her life. As a steward of God, she did not have much to give, but she gave more than those who had plenty to give. She gave from what could have been used for need, not for want.

The poor widow gave of her life to the Lord. This is how good stewards give of their time, talents, and treasures. They give everything to the Lord. So then, giving a tithe of their increase to their church is just one tenth of all they give to the Lord. One tenth is designated by the Lord to be used by those who live of the ministry. The remaining ninety percent is given by personally discerning the will of the Lord.

Giving With A Willing Heart

The most important characteristic of giving that makes a difference among God's stewards is how they give. Exodus 35:5 says of offerings given to build the tabernacle, "Take ye from among you an offering unto the LORD: whosoever is of a willing heart, let him bring it, an offering of the LORD; gold, and silver, and brass...." Exodus 25:2 says, "Speak unto the children of Israel, that they bring me an offering: of every man that giveth it willingly with his heart ye shall take my offering."

Second Corinthians 9:7 says, "Every man according as he purposeth in his heart, so let him give; not grudgingly, or of necessity: for God loveth a cheerful giver." Giving a tithe to your church is just one part of giving. Giving the remaining ninety percent to the Lord should be done just as cheerfully.

The Ministry Of Giving Help

After describing how the churches in Macedonia gave of themselves to the Lord and to those who ministered to them, Paul wrote in 2 Corinthians 8:7, "Therefore, as ye abound in every thing, in faith, and utterance, and knowledge, and in all diligence, and in your love to us, see that ye abound in this grace also." The grace spoken of in this verse is the grace of helping others financially.

Paul continued in verses 8–9 by citing Jesus as our example of giving grace. "I speak not by commandment, but by occasion of the forwardness of others, and to prove the sincerity of your love. For ye know the grace of our Lord Jesus Christ, that, though he was rich, yet for your sakes he became poor, that ye through his poverty might be rich."

Paul's advice to help other churches was not a command from God. He suggested in verses 10–11, "And herein I give my advice: for this is expedient for you, who have begun before, not only to do, but also to be forward a year ago. Now therefore perform the doing of it; that as there was a readiness to will, so there may be a performance also out of that which ye have." Paul indicated that a year earlier the Corinthians were willing and wanting to give. Now he encouraged them to follow through with the desire.

In verse 12, Paul assures the Corinthians that, though change may have occurred in circumstances and in personal wealth, their willingness was still the same. They may not be able to give as much as they would have a year earlier, but according to their willingness, they could give whatever was appropriate. "For if there be first a willing mind, it is accepted according to that a man hath, and not according to that he hath not."

In verses 13–15, Paul explained the principle of helping in time of need and then receiving help in time of need. "For I mean not that other men be eased, and ye burdened. But by an equality, that now at this time your abundance may be a supply for their want, that their abundance also may be a supply for your want: that there may be equality. As it is written, He that had gathered much had nothing over; and he that had gathered little had no lack." Due to changes in circumstances, especially in the days of persecution, churches would sometimes lack nothing and in other times be desperate. As churches help each other, they all continue to thrive, which means the Lord's work increases.

The benefit of helping applies to families and individuals as well. Those you help today may be the ones who help you tomorrow.

The Difference Among Stewards

God gives different stewards different talents and treasures. It is not how much each steward has, but how they use their talents and treasures. The goal is to win souls and train disciples.

As stewards increase their talents and treasures, they increase their tithe and their resources to achieve the end goal. Therefore, good stewards learn to manage their ninety percent to increase their giving to the Lord.

Converting time, talent, and treasures into winning souls for the kingdom of God requires wisdom and diligence. These are necessary for increasing the resources God gives to us.

Managing Your Finances

Good stewardship requires managing income, expenses, and investments. Income is the result of work and good investments. Expenses are what you spend your money on. Investments are where you put your money with the expectation of increasing your wealth.

To manage your income, expenses, and investments, you need to keep a record of the sources of your income, what you spend money on, and what investments you are putting your money into. This record is usually called a financial statement.

Here is an example of a financial statement.

Financial Statement				JANUARY	FEBRUARY	MARCH
INCOME						
Income one						
Income two						
			Total INCOME			
EXPENSES						
TITHE						
MISSIONS						
OFFERINGS						
RENT/MORTGAGE						
UTILITY, ELECTRIC						
UTILITY, GAS						
UTILITY, WATER						
UTILITY, TELEPHONE						
GROCERIES/HOUSEHOLD						
CLOTHES						
AUTO GASOLINE						
AUTO INSURANCE						
AUTO LICENSE FEES						
AUTO REPAIR						
TAX, PERSONAL PROPERTY						
MEDICAL/HEALTH						
DEBTS						
INVESTMENT, EMERGENCY (3-6 Mo. of expenses)						
GIFTS						
INVESTMENT, AUTO (purchase price)						
INVESTMENT, HOUSE (down payment amt.)						
INVESTMENT, EDUCATION						
INVESTMENT, Health Decline & age						
INVESTMENT, Career						
INVESTMENT, Others						
PERSONAL						
RECREATION / ENTERTAINMENT						
CHARITY						
			Total EXPENSES			
MONTHLY NET						
Monthly CUMULATIVE						

A financial statement shows how much money you have to work with every week or every month. This is what you are converting from your health, wisdom, and diligence. The better your health, wisdom, and diligence are, the better your income will be. This is what you are given to work with. The more income you generate, the more you have to work with.

Remember not to compare your income with others. Income is generated by health, wisdom, and diligence. Some work harder. Some work wiser. Some work hard with wisdom. Some are given more from God.

It is important to keep in mind that, as you get older, your health will diminish. This means that you will need to rely more on the preparation you made while your health, wisdom, and diligence were much better. The wisdom in Proverbs 10:5 says, "He that gathereth in summer is a wise son: but he that sleepeth in harvest is a son that causeth shame."

Expenses can be divided into four areas. First, there are your tithes and offerings. The tithe (ten percent of income) is the minimum offering mentioned in the Bible. Giving to missions and ministry needs is your investment in the Lord's work. Second, there are necessary expenses, such as food, clothing, housing, utilities, and transportation. Third, there are your investments, in which you put money to pay for things later, such as education, a house, ministries, people, and caring for yourself. Fourth, there are expenses that are not essential to survival, such as trips to the museum, recreation, vacations, etc.

The investments will keep your money working. Good management of money ensures that your assets are always increasing in value. For this reason, investing in missions and people is included. This is investment in spiritual treasures.

Managing your finances is about controlling your finances to maximize converting your assets into spiritual treasures. Mismanaging your finances will result in lost treasures and lead to debt-bondage. Proverbs 22:7 says it is not wise to be in debt. "The rich ruleth over the poor, and the borrower is servant to the lender."

Good stewards are alert to ways Satan can put them into bondage, and they make decisions to avoid those traps. You must control your finances, or they will control you! This means that Satan will have another way to prevent you from investing in the Lord's work. Satan can divert resources that could have been used for the Lord's work to bail people out of debt and to help people out of problems resulting from mismanagement of their resources. Stewards who fail to manage their finances are a drain on the finances that could go to missions and ministries.

Financial Mastery Is An Indicator Of Spiritual Mastery

The lack of resources or having less than others is not necessarily an indication of mismanagement of finances. As mentioned before, some lack health and ability.

However, those who have wealth have learned to convert their health, wisdom, and diligence into resources that can be used for the Lord. Those who inherit wealth will increase or lose their wealth due to their health, wisdom, and diligence.

John wrote in 3 John 1:2, "Beloved, I wish above all things that thou mayest prosper and be in health, even as thy soul prospereth." Good stewards know their health is a blessing from God. They do not take for granted that their health and wisdom are dependent on God. They pray for health and wisdom.

Psalm 127:1 states, "Except the LORD build the house, they labour in vain that build it: except the LORD keep the city, the watchman waketh but in vain." Our mastery of finances is a reflection of our spirituality, as is every area of our lives. Mastery is not about how much wealth we have. It is about managing the wealth we have.

Good stewards are diligent to use their health and to apply wisdom in making good financial decisions. Proverbs 10:4 says, "He becometh poor that dealeth with a slack hand: but the hand of the diligent maketh rich." This requires being diligent to learn and understand how to manage finances.

Romans 12:11 admonishes stewards to be "not slothful in business; fervent in spirit; serving the Lord."

In contrast, Proverbs 6:9–11 warns, "How long wilt thou sleep, O sluggard? When wilt thou arise out of thy sleep? A little sleep, a little slumber, a little folding of the hands to sleep: shall thy poverty come as one that travelleth, and thy want as an armed man."

Spiritual mastery is being responsible to manage everything for the Lord. First Corinthians 10:31 says, "Whether therefore ye eat, or drink, or whatsoever ye do, do all to the glory of God." First Timothy 5:8 warns about being irresponsible, saying, "But if any provide not for his own, and specially for those of his own house, he hath denied the faith, and is worse than an infidel."

6

GOOD STEWARDS BUILD GOOD RELATIONSHIPS

A good steward invests time, talent, and treasures into relationships and learns how to protect those relationships. Paul wrote that all Christians are ambassadors of Jesus Christ and have the responsibility to help others reconcile with God. "Now then we are ambassadors for Christ, as though God did beseech you by us: we pray you in Christ's stead, be ye reconciled to God" (2 Corinthians 5:20). Reconciliation of relationships means that Christians should be expert at building, sustaining, and restoring relationships.

The Problem With Anger

We live in a world of anger and division. Anger is the norm, and it is condoned in our culture. It is glamorized and encouraged. But anger does not build good relationships.

Our culture has reached a place where anger is accepted as a good emotional expression. Articles have been published touting how beneficial it is to express anger. But anger is not a virtue. Anger is an emotional expression of carnality. Anger is sin. The

Bible warns in Ephesians 4:26, "Be ye angry, and sin not: let not the sun go down upon your wrath."

How is it possible to be angry and not sin? Injustice will provoke anger. This is righteous anger. But anger must be controlled, and because we are exhorted to resolve our anger by the end of the day, anger can be controlled.

Romans 12:17–21 says, "Recompense to no man evil for evil. Provide things honest in the sight of all men. If it be possible, as much as lieth in you, live peaceably with all men. Dearly beloved, avenge not yourselves, but rather give place unto wrath: for it is written, Vengeance is mine; I will repay, saith the Lord. Therefore if thine enemy hunger, feed him; if he thirst, give him drink: for in so doing thou shalt heap coals of fire on his head. Be not overcome of evil, but overcome evil with good."

The problem with anger is that it makes you feel justified to lash out and hurt others. Despite how justified you may feel and how clearly you seem to understand the wrong you are angry about, anger hurts. Anger damages relationships. Verbal abuse and physical abuse are not okay.

Everyone knows what anger feels like. Anger is an emotional state provoked by offense or loss. People can be angry about people, events, or at things. Someone may make a comment or do something that causes offense. Anger can be triggered because plans and goals are not happening. Anger may be triggered by pain due to accidentally slipping.

Anger must and can be controlled. There is no excuse for not resolving anger. Self-control is better than being out of control. Talking peaceably is better than talking angrily. Good stewards control their anger for the purpose of building good and lasting relationships with people.

Three Essentials For Good Relationships

Being trustworthy, knowing how to reconcile when offense occurs, and expressing love are the three essentials to great relationships. Trustworthiness is how others think about you. Love is what you do for others. Reconciliation is what you must do to restore trust. These three things are necessary for building and nurturing relationships with others.

Trust Is What Others Think About You

Trust is what others think and feel about you. When you are consistent in showing that you care about others, that others can count on you to be helpful, and that you do not want to do them any harm, they will trust you. If you are inconsistent in showing that you are trustworthy, then people will not trust you.

Winning the trust of others requires that you be consistent and predictable in what you say and do. People protect themselves from harm, and they must have confidence that you will not mistreat them or betray them. In a world of sin and Satan, people must protect themselves. There are many tragedies occurring every day because people hurt others. Do you hurt people or help to heal them?

Are you reliable? Are you dependable? Can people count on you not to hurt them or disappoint them? Do you assure people they can have confidence in you by the way you act and by the things you do? Actions need to back up your words.

Do you make excuses for being irresponsible? Do you find yourself apologizing often for your failure to fulfill promises and responsibilities? If so, you are letting people know that you are unreliable. Excuses let people know they cannot count on you to do the things you promise to do.

The Sadness Of Not Finding Someone To Trust

People look for people they can trust. Some, after repeatedly being hurt, stop trusting. This means they must always guard themselves from hurt. Some stop trusting everyone. They never feel safe around others. They feel afraid and nervous. They live with anxiety. Their guard is always up and they cannot relax when they are around people.

This is a sad state to be in. People who cannot trust others live under constant stress. They must be suspicious of everyone. There is no feeling of peace and rest. They feel rejected and alone. This creates a self-centered and selfish perspective. Fortunately, we can always trust Jesus to love us and care for us.

The Benefits Of Trust

Trust is essential for happy relationships. Proverbs 31:11 says, "The heart of her husband doth safely trust in her, so that he shall have no need of spoil." When you trust someone, you are happy and comforted in heart and mind. This is what people want, and the benefit of being able to trust someone applies to everyone, not just husbands.

Being able to trust someone makes us feel safe and secure. We are comforted by being able to trust others to protect us and to treat us right. We are strengthened emotionally.

How To Be Trustworthy

Good stewards create safe environments where people feel they can relax and not be afraid of being betrayed. Colossians 3:8–10 says, "But now ye also put off all these; anger, wrath, malice, blasphemy, filthy communication out of your mouth. Lie not one to another, seeing that ye have put off the old man with his deeds;

And have put on the new man, which is renewed in knowledge after the image of him that created him."

To teach others about the trustworthiness of Christ, we should be examples of being trustworthy. As disciples of Jesus Christ, we should represent how much He values honesty, justice, and responsibility. Whether people trust us or not, we should not be giving them reasons to doubt us or God.

God's consistency in being dependable and loving shows us He is trustworthy. Likewise, it is important that we be consistent in our Christlikeness. If we are unpredictable and careless about how we treat others, people will have difficulty in trusting us.

Anger, deceit, cursing, and stealing are qualities and behaviors in people that make others distrust them. These are not characteristics of Christ, and they should not characterize those who claim to be Christians.

Do good to others, be helpful, and encourage them to do well in their lives. Galatians 6:10 says, "As we have therefore opportunity, let us do good unto all men, especially unto them who are of the household of faith."

Reconciliation Restores Trust

Jesus said in Matthew 18:7 that offense will come. "Woe unto the world because of offences! for it must needs be that offences come; but woe to that man by whom the offence cometh!"

Everyone has been offended and will be offended. It is a part of living with others. Sometimes offenses are unintentional, but the hurt is just as real and hurtful as intentional offenses.

Proverbs 28:26 explains, "He that trusteth in his own heart is a fool: but whoso walketh wisely, he shall be delivered." If we cannot trust our own hearts, then it is inevitable that we will say things or do things that offend others.

Offense is the feeling you have after being wrongly accused, treated unfairly, or judged unjustly. You are hurt and perhaps angry as well. Offense is a violation of trust and a threat to your personal well-being and security. It is an attack on your reputation that you consider undeserved and wrong.

Offense is a breach of trust. When you do something or say something that is deemed unfair or unjust, others will doubt that your judgment is trustworthy. When you offend others, they will feel and think of your motives and judgment as a personal attack and a threat to their safety and security. When you do something that people perceive to be unjust and unloving, their trust in you is damaged. They are offended.

Avoid Causing Offense

Offense is due to being defrauded. This means to feel you have been treated unfairly and unjustly. Though offense is unavoidable, good stewards attempt to avoid offending others by showing respect. Romans 12:18 says, "If it be possible, as much as lieth in you, live peaceably with all men."

Second Corinthians 6:3 admonishes, "Giving no offence in any thing, that the ministry be not blamed." A trustworthy message requires trustworthy messengers. A message of peace should be brought in peace. A message asking for trust should be delivered by trustworthy messengers. A ministry of reconciliation requires messengers who avoid causing offense and who reconcile quickly if offense does occur.

First Thessalonians 4:6 says, "That no man go beyond and defraud his brother in any matter." Good stewards show respect and avoid offending others. They give the appropriate honor to whom honor is due.

First Corinthians 7:5 admonishes, "Defraud ye not one the other, except it be with consent for a time, that ye may give yourselves to fasting and prayer; and come together again, that Satan tempt you not for your incontinency." Regardless of the relationship, defrauding another causes hurt. Hurt people will become defensive, withdrawn, and possibly angry. This prevents relationships from being wholesome and close.

Treat people with respect, use respectful language, be kind, be helpful, and show the honor that is due to them. Be a trustworthy friend. Fulfill your promises, be reliable, and be encouraging. Can you imagine if everyone treated you this way, and you treated everyone else this way? People would be happy, helpful, and trusting. This is the kind of world God wants us to live in.

Reconcile Every Offense

James 3:2 says, "For in many things we offend all. If any man offend not in word, the same is a perfect man, and able also to bridle the whole body." Someday we will be perfect, will never offend others, and will live in the wholesome environment of heaven. But until then, we need to learn how to reconcile.

Reconciliation is the duty of every Christian. Spiritually, believers are ambassadors of Jesus Christ in the world. Our role is to reconcile people with God. Second Corinthians 5:18–20 says, "And all things are of God, who hath reconciled us to himself by Jesus Christ, and hath given to us the ministry of reconciliation; To wit, that God was in Christ, reconciling the world unto himself, not imputing their trespasses unto them; and hath committed unto us the word of reconciliation. Now then we are ambassadors for Christ, as though God did beseech you by us: we pray you in Christ's stead, be ye reconciled to God." To reconcile others with God, believers need to know how to reconcile with others. Open, trusting conversation about God requires a good relationship.

The Responsibility Of The Offender

Regardless of the reason people are offended, they are hurt, and the natural tendency is to withdraw. They may be offended for legitimate reasons, or they may be offended due to a misunderstanding.

Withdrawing from someone who has hurt you leads to a breakdown in communication. Conversations become guarded and minimized. Avoiding confrontation when being in the presence of the offender is safer.

The natural tendency to withdraw from a hurtful relationship is understandable. For this reason, it is expected of the offender to reach out to the person they have offended. Jesus taught in Matthew 5:23-24, "Therefore if thou bring thy gift to the altar, and there rememberest that thy brother hath ought against thee; Leave there thy gift before the altar, and go thy way; first be reconciled to thy brother, and then come and offer thy gift." It is reasonable to expect the offender to approach the person offended due to the protective response to withdraw. It is easier for the offender to approach the offended.

Sometimes, both sides in a disagreement feel offended. This makes reconciliation more difficult. But good stewards keep in mind that it is more important to serve God than to consider their own personal feelings. Good stewards have a good relationship with God and are strengthened by God to seek reconciliation. For this reason, Jesus requires those who worship Him to first reconcile with those they have offended.

A good steward will usually be sensitive enough to know they have hurt someone and have caused offense. But sometimes, people unintentionally offend, or sometimes the offended has misunderstood the real intent of something said or done.

In Matthew 18:15, Jesus said, "Moreover if thy brother shall trespass against thee, go and tell him his fault between thee and him alone: if he shall hear thee, thou hast gained thy brother." If an offense is not dealt with by the offender, the offended should make the offender aware of the problem. A misunderstanding or unintentional offense can be quickly resolved and trust restored.

Reconciliation When Intentional Offense Occurs

In the event the offender has intentionally tried to hurt another, it is appropriate to confront the offender. If the offender is stubborn and resistant to the Spirit of God, Jesus said in Matthew 18:16, "But if he will not hear thee, then take with thee one or two more, that in the mouth of two or three witnesses every word may be established."

The goal is to reconcile, not to escalate the conflict. Good stewards enlist the help of others to bring reconciliation rather than to worsen the conflict.

In such cases, the decision to reconcile is up to the offender. It is the offender's responsibility to reconcile with the offended first. If he/she does not seek reconciliation, then the offended can choose to seek reconciliation. However, the offender will still make the decision whether reconciliation will occur.

Reconciliation Is Necessary For Message Credibility

Because reconciliation is such a vital part of our ministry for God, Jesus considers reconciliation imperative in His church. In

Matthew 18:17, Jesus said, "And if he shall neglect to hear them, tell it unto the church: but if he neglect to hear the church, let him be unto thee as an heathen man and a publican."

Members in churches should understand their roles as ambassadors of Jesus Christ. To reconcile the world with Christ requires that the messengers of Christ's message be trustworthy.

Those who are not concerned about reconciling with others or about the effect discord has on the credibility of the church's ministry should not be members of a church. Jesus said members who prefer to create a hostile and untrustworthy atmosphere should not be associated with His church. If they decide to repent, they would be welcomed back. Reconciliation would be appropriate. This is the message of Christ.

The Spirit Of Reconciliation

The Spirit of God is working in the world to bring others to Christ. He confirms the message of peace with God in the hearts of humanity. This spirit of peace should be manifested in the servants of Christ. The absence of peace in a message is evidence that a believer is not being led by the Spirit of God. Second Timothy 1:7 says, "For God hath not given us the spirit of fear; but of power, and of love, and of a sound mind."

James 3:14–18 describes the mind and heart of those under the influence of the Spirit of God. "But if ye have bitter envying and strife in your hearts, glory not, and lie not against the truth. This wisdom descendeth not from above, but is earthly, sensual, devilish. But the wisdom that is from above is first pure, then peaceable, gentle, and easy to be intreated, full of mercy and good fruits, without partiality, and without hypocrisy. And the fruit of righteousness is sown in peace of them that make peace."

Good stewards are easy to talk to and are easy to work with when resolving offenses because they are under the influence of the Spirit of God. Beware when you feel anger and strife in your heart. You are not being led by the Spirit of God. The Spirit of God is conducting a ministry of reconciliation, not contention.

How To Reconcile With The Offended

In a world of sin and rebellion, many refuse to reconcile. If they refuse to reconcile with God, it should be no surprise that reconciliation with people is refused as well. Pride causes offense, and pride prevents reconciliation.

Humility is necessary for reconciliation and peace. Psalm 119:165 says, "Great peace have they which love thy law: and nothing shall offend them." The humility of good stewards of God allows them to live in peace with God and to seek peace with others. Their humility allows them to be willing to reconcile.

Because offense is a breach of trust, it is important to reconcile by restoring trust. This requires an apology and assurance that the offense will not happen again. The apology humbly acknowledges wrong has been done. Assurance is necessary to restore trust.

It is understood that people are flawed and prone to repeat their mistakes. But to restore trust, a commitment to stop the offense is necessary. There should be assurance that earnest effort will be made to prevent future offense. Without assurance, the cause of the offense will not be resolved. There is no reason to be trusted.

How To Reconcile With The Offender

It is easier to reconcile with an offender who apologizes and gives assurance that he/she will try not to offend again. There is an effort on the offender's part to restore trust.

But how do people reconcile when both feel offended by the other or when the offender does not feel he/she has done wrong? Who should apologize and give assurance?

Reconciliation is the goal. This means the goal is to establish a peaceable relationship. Both offended parties can apologize for unintended offense and give assurance that they will avoid offending now that they understand the problem.

If someone believes he/she is doing no wrong and continues to offend, this individual must be treated as one who refuses to reconcile. Counsel with two or three other godly stewards is necessary. The goal is to resolve offenses, not to escalate them. In counsel, it may be discovered that there is no basis for the offense. Then the offended person must be counseled to understand the perceived offense with the right perspective.

In some cases, two people may have to agree to disagree and leave it up to God to resolve the problem. In this case, they should pray for each other and for themselves. God's mission for their lives is more important than the problem. The problem must be sacrificed for the sake of God's mission. It must be resolved by the people involved or given to the Lord to resolve, in which case both parties must be content to let the Lord handle the problem.

Nonetheless, an unresolved offense is a breach of trust. Good stewards realize that this breach of trust weakens relationships, which compromises the mission of God. In this case, people need to be careful to control their attitudes, pray for peace, and be aware of the spirit that is controlling them.

Living Without Offense

Jesus said that offense is inevitable. This is due to pride and selfishness. Though we are born again spiritually, the flesh is still carnal and tempted to sin. Good stewards control their carnal impulses and yield to the way of the Spirit.

When we yield to the Spirit, it is possible to live without offense. Paul said in Acts 24:16, "And herein do I exercise myself, to have always a conscience void of offence toward God, and toward men." This does not mean that others will not be offended by you. People were offended by Jesus, and they crucified Him. People were offended by Paul's message, and he was killed. Jesus said in Luke 10:16, "He that heareth you heareth me; and he that despiseth you despiseth me; and he that despiseth me despiseth him that sent me."

Living without offense is the attitude of good stewards. In a ministry of reconciliation, good stewards understand that being mistreated and despised for being Christian is a rejection of Christ. For this reason, good stewards are not personally offended. They have made their choice to serve Christ, and they recognize the right of others to reject Christ.

The choices people make are between them and God. Stewards are the messengers. There is nothing to be offended by.

Love For Good Relationships

Whereas trust is the confidence others have in you, love is the commitment you have for others. Love is the reason you desire to be trustworthy and to gain the trust of others. Love is the reason you desire to build new relationships. Love is the reason you humble yourself for the sake of reconciliation with others. Love is the reason you desire to do good and not evil to others. Love is the reason you desire to be a good steward.

Love is the reason you desire to fulfill the admonition of Colossians 3:23, "And whatsoever ye do, do it heartily, as to the Lord, and not unto men." When you love God with all your heart, soul, and mind, you desire to participate in the mission He has given you. This mission is to win souls and train disciples, using whatever gifts and skills you have. This mission is about building good relationships.

A community of believers who strive to be good stewards is a community that is wholesome, nurturing, safe, and encouraging. They provoke one another unto love and good works, which is the admonition of Hebrews 10:24, "And let us consider one another to provoke unto love and to good works."

This admonition is followed by the encouragement to assemble. Hebrews 10:25 says, "Not forsaking the assembling of ourselves together, as the manner of some is; but exhorting one another: and so much the more, as ye see the day approaching."

Love is about building relationships. Churches are communities of believers who assemble to encourage each other in the Lord. They nurture their relationships and build a community of loving believers who will win more souls and train disciples in the love of Christ. Relationships cannot happen without time spent together. Churches cannot fulfill their mission without good relationships.

Good stewards are relationship experts. Their love for God compels them to build relationships with other believers and to reconcile others with God. They share their love for God by showing love for others.

Love For Reconciliation

If offenses are not resolved, trust is not possible. Offenders are deemed untrustworthy. Relationships break down, and ministry is damaged. Good stewards realize that they must be vigilant to sustain good relationships.

God's love is enduring. Human love is fickle. For this reason, it is important to nurture your love for God. With God's enduring love, your love for others will be more enduring.

God's love compelled Him to sacrifice Himself to make reconciliation with us possible. His love will compel us to do likewise. When offense occurs, in the love of God we will humble ourselves to make reconciliation our top priority. After all, we are ministers of reconciliation (2 Corinthians 5:18–19).

Loving Others With God's Love

God's love is sacrificial and permanent. It endures all things for the sake of establishing relationships. The Bible distinguishes God's love by calling it charity, which is translated from *agape*. This *agape* love is described in 1 Corinthians 13:4–7, "Charity suffereth long, and is kind; charity envieth not; charity vaunteth not itself, is not puffed up, Doth not behave itself unseemly, seeketh not her own, is not easily provoked, thinketh no evil; Rejoiceth not in iniquity, but rejoiceth in the truth; Beareth all things, believeth all things, hopeth all things, endureth all things."

The qualities of love described in this passage are qualities manifested in those who nurture their love for God. They are qualities that make for good relationships.

Love is patient, kind, humble, unselfish, not easily offended, honest, tolerant, and hopeful. It is not mean, envious, proud, arrogant, selfish, malevolent, and sinful.

Love is what makes good relationships possible. Love compels us to build others up, to be helpful, to be encouraging, to rejoice when others do well, succeed, and improve themselves.

A loving environment is safe. People trust each other and protect each other. They help each other become better in all that they do.

Love compels us with the desire to protect and repair relationships. Love is vital to reconciliation because it gives a reason to forgive when we are offended.

First Corinthians 13:4–7 says that love "beareth all things, believeth all things, hopeth all things, endureth all things." These four qualities of love make reconciliation possible. Because of love for another, we are willing to tolerate offenses. When someone proves themselves to be untrustworthy, we are hopeful and still believe they can be helped and that the relationship can be restored. In other words, the love of God does not abandon hope for reconciliation. And regardless of the problems, love will endure. God's love will always outlast problems.

We need God's love in us to endure all things and to not give up on hope for reconciling a broken relationship. God does not give up on us. We should not give up on others.

Love And Forgiveness

Forgiveness is about showing mercy and not seeking vengeance. It is about releasing the feelings of vengeance, hate, and meanness that come with offense.

Showing the love of God requires showing forgiveness. Can you imagine talking about the love of God without including forgiveness? It is not possible. God forgives because He loves. There is no sin God will not forgive before you die. He wants reconciliation and peace. This is what we need to desire as well. We should be as willing as God is to forgive. Peace and reconciliation should be hallmarks of our testimonies as Christians.

Forgiving Chronic Offenders

As often as a person repents, God is willing to forgive. In Luke 17:3-4, Jesus taught, "Take heed to yourselves: If thy brother trespass against thee, rebuke him; and if he repent, forgive him. And if he trespass against thee seven times in a day, and seven times in a day turn again to thee, saying, I repent; thou shalt forgive him."

Repentance is a change of mind. It is a change in what you believe. Offenders are repentant when they change their mind about doing wrong and want to do right.

Some struggle with consistency. Sometimes they want to do right, and sometimes they want to do wrong. They can sincerely repent to do right one moment and change their mind again and not want to do right. This is the way of humanity. First John 1:8 says, "If we say that we have no sin, we deceive ourselves, and the truth is not in us." For this reason, Christians are constantly asking for God's forgiveness.

As long as a person repents, we should forgive. This is what Christ does, and this is what we must do for a ministry of reconciliation.

Forgiving Dangerous Offenders

At some point, chronic offenders, especially those who are abusive, divisive, and a threat to the well-being of the community, must be avoided. Titus 3:10 says, "A man that is an heretick after the first and second admonition reject." Romans 16:17 admonishes, "Now I beseech you, brethren, mark them which cause divisions and offences contrary to the doctrine which ye have learned; and avoid them." There are different types of offenses and different degrees of risk associated with different offenses. However, there is a common way to think about all offenses that could cause harm spiritually or physically.

Being forgiving does not mean putting yourself or others at risk. We should always desire the best for everyone, including the wicked. We should always be eager to forgive and reconcile differences. But we must also be careful to protect ourselves and others.

Jesus said most will not repent (Matthew 7:13–14). And John 2:24–25 says, "But Jesus did not commit himself unto them, because he knew all men, And needed not that any should testify of man: for he knew what was in man." We must always be cautious to protect ourselves. Though being a Christian often comes with persecution, God does not require that we deliberately put ourselves in harm's way.

If there is reason to suspect someone will do you harm, you should protect yourself. You are not obligated to put yourself at risk. Good stewards protect themselves and others. And though you may forgive someone of a dangerous offense, you may have reason not to trust that person.

Is it possible to love and forgive someone who is untrustworthy? Is it possible to be both forgiving and cautious at the same time? Second Thessalonians 3:14-15 says, "And if any man obey not our word by this epistle, note that man, and have no company with him, that he may be ashamed. Yet count him not as an enemy, but admonish him as a brother." Avoiding close fellowship with a dangerous offender is necessary in order to avoid being hurt or influenced to stray from God. But the distancing should be done in love, to protect, and not to be mean, hateful, and spiteful.

The Christ-like heart for reconciliation seeks resolution. But having this attitude does not require subjecting yourself to harm or putting your spirituality at risk before or after repentance and forgiveness.

Degrees Of Trust

Some people are chronically untrustworthy. They can be well-meaning most of the time, and sincerely repentant sometimes, and capable of being kind when they feel like it. The problem is they are unpredictable. This makes them untrustworthy.

Some offenses are more dangerous than others. Some offenders are more predictable than others. For these reasons, one must have wisdom to determine how much to trust others. Some can be trusted with your life. Others can never be trusted to do anything important. And still others can be trusted only for certain things.

The decision to trust is yours to make. The offender has no right to tell the offended they should trust the offender. Regardless of the reason for trusting an untrustworthy person, if harm is done, the offended made the decision to trust and will learn to be more cautious.

Love hopes for reconciliation and believes reconciliation is possible for all people. But we also know that many choose not to repent and do not intend to be kind. Only God knows the true state of repentance and what a person really thinks. There are offenders who are dangerous deceivers, and others who are sincere but unreliable. We must ask God for wisdom to discern whom to trust and how much to trust.

Psalm 118:8 says, "It is better to trust in the LORD than to put confidence in man." It is not surprising that everyone can be guilty of disappointing others. But some are more untrustworthy than others.

Conditional Forgiveness

As mentioned above, Jesus said in Luke 17:3-4, "If he repent, forgive him." God forgives those who repent.

Second Chronicles 7:14 says, "If my people, which are called by my name, shall humble themselves, and pray, and seek my face, and turn from their wicked ways; then will I hear from heaven, and will forgive their sin, and will heal their land."

In Luke 13:5, Jesus said, "I tell you, Nay: but, except ye repent, ye shall all likewise perish." God forgives only if there is repentance.

Refusing to forgive someone who is not repentant does not justify being mean and spiteful. Being unforgiving must be done with the attitude of God. He is always willing to forgive. He does not desire that any perish. He does not desire that any should suffer. He always loves and always offers forgiveness. Reconciliation is the goal. But reconciliation requires repentance from the offender as well as forgiveness from the offended.

Though God forgives only those who repent, He is still loving, kind, and willing to forgive. Romans 5:8 says, "But God commendeth his love toward us, in that, while we were yet sinners, Christ died for us." It is possible to be loving and kind to the unrepentant. Good stewards demonstrate their love by having the desire and making the effort to help the unrepentant reconcile with God and others.

Forgiveness And Justice

One of the first concerns people have with forgiveness is the thought of allowing crimes to go unpunished. But forgiveness is not about ignoring justice. God is forgiving, and He is just. He makes things right. This is justice.

It is right to forgive, and it is right to be just. To do right and restore trusting relationships requires forgiveness, repentance, and justice.

True repentance will produce a desire to make things right, which is important to reconciliation. The offended should look for evidence of true repentance from the offender. The offender should show a willingness to assure the offended that the repentance is genuine.

An offender who repents of having done wrong will be willing to make things right. Luke 19:8 records the story of a tax collector who repented of dishonestly gaining wealth. "And Zacchaeus stood, and said unto the Lord; Behold, Lord, the half of my goods I give to the poor; and if I have taken any thing from any man by false accusation, I restore him fourfold." Zacchaeus repented and desired to make things right.

In some cases, justice can only be achieved by surrendering to the authorities. God set up governments to protect communities from crime and violence. Everyone knows the rules, and those who engage in criminal activity should expect to take their punishment as determined by the laws of the community. For example, murderers and rapists who repent will surrender to the authorities.

Desiring justice is not wrong. It is the right desire. Tolerating and condoning injustice is not right. Allowing crimes to go unpunished creates an atmosphere of distrust, insecurity, and unrighteousness. This is not consistent with having a ministry of reconciliation. Reconciliation restores trust, peace, and security.

Good stewards uphold justice and righteousness with the goal of reconciling people with God and each other. They are always willing to be forgiving and to reconcile.

Forgiveness Is Important For Your Spiritual Well-being

Forgiveness is important for your spiritual well-being. It protects you from being controlled by evil thoughts. It keeps you focused on following the Spirit of God and pursuing His desire to reconcile everyone with God. It shows that the desire you have for God is greater than your desire for vengeance and harm.

As mentioned before, James 3:14–16 warns, "But if ye have bitter envying and strife in your hearts, glory not, and lie not against the truth. This wisdom descendeth not from above, but is earthly, sensual, devilish. For where envying and strife is, there is confusion and every evil work." To be a good steward of God, it is important not to succumb to the passions of hate, anger, and vengeance. These passions make you vulnerable to being confused about what is right and just. You will be in danger of being overcome by evil, giving in to evil thoughts, attitudes, and behaviors.

When you are offended, turn to the Lord for wisdom and guidance to discover what to do. Remember three things. First, God is always willing to forgive you. Second, the Spirit of God is willing to forgive everyone. You should do no less. Third, you will recognize the Spirit of God guiding you by the peace you have with God.

James 3:17–18 says, "But the wisdom that is from above is first pure, then peaceable, gentle, and easy to be intreated, full of mercy and good fruits, without partiality, and without hypocrisy. And the fruit of righteousness is sown in peace of them that make peace."

The Spirit of God is working in the world to bring peace in relationships, first with God. This is an important attitude and perspective to have as Christians. We represent Jesus Christ, not ourselves.

Forgiving others is a ministry of remembering what Christ did for us. He does not harbor resentment. He forgave us of our sins and showed us mercy and grace. We should always be willing to forgive those who offend us.

Forgiveness Is Important For Your Ministry Of Reconciliation

Forgiveness demonstrates through our examples God's willingness to reconcile despite having been wronged. Colossians 3:13 says, "Forbearing one another, and forgiving one another, if any man have a quarrel against any: even as Christ forgave you, so also do ye." If God was willing to forgive us, then, as His stewards, we should be forgiving as well. Likewise, if God is willing to forgive those who offend us, we should be willing to do no less.

Christians are called to be ministers of reconciliation. Therefore, you should show the desire for reconciliation. You should always be willing to forgive. You should always desire to pray for everyone to be reconciled with God and to experience salvation. First Peter 3:9 says, "Not rendering evil for evil, or railing for railing: but contrariwise blessing; knowing that ye are thereunto called, that ye should inherit a blessing." First Thessalonians 5:15 says, "See that none render evil for evil unto any man; but ever follow that which is good, both among yourselves, and to all men."

Good stewards seek to do good to everyone. Everything they do should be consistent with trying to achieve peace and blessings for everyone. If your attitudes, words, and actions do not align with God's goal of reconciling the world with Him, then you are not fulfilling God's will, and your testimony as a minister of reconciliation is contradicted. It is important to be forgiving.

Love Is Important For Good Relationships

John 3:16 says, "For God so loved the world, that he gave his only begotten Son, that whosoever believeth in him should not perish, but have everlasting life." God's love compels Him to seek reconciliation. His love is the reason He sacrificed His Son for our benefit. First John 4:10 says, "Herein is love, not that we loved God, but that he loved us, and sent his Son to be the propitiation for our sins." He loves us. And because of His love, we are His friends.

When we love God with all our hearts, souls, and minds, we too will love others. When His love rules in our hearts, we will have the same desires He has. Helping others become friends with God will be our primary goal. We will arrange everything else in our lives around achieving that goal.

Because of love, we will desire to be friends with others and to show them God's love. We will show love by being trustworthy, avoiding offense, and being ready to forgive and reconcile.

Love is like healing salve on wounds. First Peter 4:8 says, "And above all things have fervent charity among yourselves: for charity shall cover the multitude of sins." Love makes reconciliation possible. It makes repentance possible. It makes forgiveness possible. And it makes trust possible.

God's love makes it possible for us to love our enemies. Luke 6:27 says, "But I say unto you which hear, Love your enemies, do good to them which hate you." Love seeks to make things right, regardless of what others want to do. God is always loving, and we should always be loving, regardless of what others do.

In Matthew 5:38–39, Jesus said, "Ye have heard that it hath been said, An eye for an eye, and a tooth for a tooth: But I say unto you, That ye resist not evil: but whosoever shall smite thee on thy right cheek, turn to him the other also."

Jesus is saying not to resist evil with evil. Rather, we should continue to show His love for our enemies even though they offend us and tempt us to do evil. Jesus is not teaching that believers should forsake righteousness and justice. He is saying we should choose God's way, not the way of evil. Do not deviate from doing right to respond to evil. Continue doing what is right. Seek peace with the desire to make things right, to seek justice, to be forgiving, and to pursue reconciliation.

We do not want to be as those who reject God's ways. We want to show that God's way is good, perfect, and acceptable. Romans 12:2 says, "And be not conformed to this world: but be ye transformed by the renewing of your mind, that ye may prove what is that good, and acceptable, and perfect, will of God." The way you choose to go is the way you believe is right. Will you follow the way of your enemies or the way of God?

7

GOOD STEWARDS CREATE A CULTURE OF ENHANCEMENT

Good stewards create an environment of enhancement around them. As they strive to improve their personal stewardship, they also strive to improve the stewardship of others. As their disciples strive to improve, they enhance the environment with energy to improve serving the Lord.

In a church setting, good stewards help each other with experience, wisdom, talents, and treasures. A growing, thriving network develops, and everyone is better because of the positive, forward momentum that is created by stewards striving to improve themselves.

A chain reaction of enhancement takes place from one disciple to the other. But the atmosphere of enhancement in the church also enhances the leaders, not just those becoming leaders. It is a culture that stimulates spiritual growth and wise investment in others, and one that wins more souls.

8

GOOD STEWARDS LIVE THE ABUNDANT LIFE

In John 10:10, Jesus said, "The thief cometh not, but for to steal, and to kill, and to destroy: I am come that they might have life, and that they might have it more abundantly."

An abundant life is a life that is superior to all other options and exceeds expectations. The abundant life promised by Jesus begins with eternal life. Eternal life is never ending. It lasts forever. Nothing will exceed the life offered by Jesus.

The abundant life of Jesus is a life of fulfillment, contentment, peace with God, wisdom from God, hope for a better future, riches in heaven, joyfulness for God's blessings, and participation in the greatest purpose in creation.

Jesus came to save souls. In Luke 19:10, Jesus said, "For the Son of man is come to seek and to save that which was lost." The most important thing that can happen to anyone is to experience salvation from eternal death and condemnation.

In Matthew 28:19–20, Jesus commissioned His church to continue His work. "Go ye therefore, and teach all nations, baptizing them in the name of the Father, and of the Son, and of the Holy Ghost:

Teaching them to observe all things whatsoever I have commanded you: and, lo, I am with you alway, even unto the end of the world. Amen."

Every Christian is called to represent Jesus Christ as His ambassador and steward. Second Corinthians 5:17–20 says, "Therefore if any man be in Christ, he is a new creature: old things are passed away; behold, all things are become new. And all things are of God, who hath reconciled us to himself by Jesus Christ, and hath given to us the ministry of reconciliation; To wit, that God was in Christ, reconciling the world unto himself, not imputing their trespasses unto them; and hath committed unto us the word of reconciliation. Now then we are ambassadors for Christ, as though God did beseech you by us: we pray you in Christ's stead, be ye reconciled to God."

Christians have a never-ending life with purpose that exceeds the dead-end, self-serving life of the lost. Christians serve God with a higher purpose. They are elevated in their purpose and status with God. This is something God wants everyone to enjoy. Jesus came to give the abundant life. He offers it to everyone. All they must do is believe His way is the right way.

I hope you have made the choice to be a good steward to God. The rewards are out of this world. The experiences are supernatural. And the sense of fulfillment is unmatched.

Continue your training to be a good steward. Follow Christ. Be a disciple that will make a difference in the world and help others make life changing choices for good.

9

GOOD STEWARDS ANSWER QUESTIONS ABOUT STEWARDSHIP

1. Why is the wicked and slothful servant spoken of in Matthew 25:14–30 cast into outer darkness where there will be weeping and gnashing of teeth? The unprofitable servant represents the lost. God's desire and plan is for everyone to believe in Him and to serve Him as profitable servants. Those who choose not to believe in Him will be condemned. It is the choice they make, believing their way is better than God's way.

2. When will the Lord return? No one knows. Jesus said He did not know (Matthew 24:36). Only the Father in heaven knows. We are in the last days right now (Acts 2:17), so we should live with a sense of urgency and be prepared for His return (Colossians 4:5; 2 Corinthians 6:2).

3. What does it mean to be judged by fire in 1 Corinthians 3:13? Fire refers to judgment by God. There is a judgment of the lost and a judgment of the saved. First Corinthians 3:11–15 describes how Christians will be judged. They will be judged for their works, for rewards or for loss. First Corinthians 3:15 clearly states that they will still be saved.

This judgment is not for the salvation or condemnation of their souls.

4. What are the consequences of not loving God first of all with all my heart, soul, and mind? As a steward, you have been given talents to use for God's purpose. If you do not use them for Him, you will lose the rewards you could have had. Though you will be saved, there will be loss.

5. Is it sinful to try to gain heavenly rewards? No. Jesus told about the rewards and treasures in heaven and exhorted us to strive for the treasures that are in heaven rather than those on earth (Luke 12:33–34).

6. To be content, should I not seek to improve my life, career, and wealth? No. Being content is being thankful to God for what you have. Discontentment is being unthankful. Seeking to improve your life should be for the purpose of increasing your talents for God. He expects wise investments to be made to increase for His glory.

7. If I am not winning souls to Christ for salvation, am I being an unprofitable servant? First, a servant is judged by what he chooses to do. He is not judged by what others choose to do. A good steward uses his time, talents, and treasures to win souls, whether those souls respond favorably or not. First Corinthians 4:2 says, "Moreover it is required in stewards, that a man be found faithful." Second, you may not personally be engaged in leading souls to the Lord, but good stewards help those who are.

8. Is it possible to give too much money to my church ministries and missionaries? No. All your money is God's. You are His steward. Use your money wisely to advance His cause. Invest your money to increase the number of souls that will be saved.

10

GOOD STEWARDS TEACH OTHERS HOW TO BE GOOD STEWARDS

Prepare Yourself

- Pray. Ask God to give you wisdom and to help you love Him with all your heart, soul, and mind.
- Read. Read verses and examples in the Bible about stewardship to God.
- Study. Refer to the verses in this book to help you study stewardship.
- Meditate. Take time to be thoughtful about how to be a good steward to God.
- Be confident. The Lord wants His disciples to share His message with others. He will help you as you share His Word.

Organize Your Lesson Topics

1. What does Jesus consider a good steward to be?

- Good stewards are prepared for His return.

- Good stewards will be rewarded with heavenly treasures.
- Bad stewards will suffer loss.
- Good stewards stay focused on serving God.

2. Stewards manage the resources given to them by God for God.

- Good stewards rely on God and His wisdom.
- Good stewards do God's will.
- Good stewards are thankful for God's gifts of time, talents, and treasures.
- Good stewards invest their resources into reconciling souls to Christ.
- Good stewards invest in others to increase God's resources through people.
- Good stewards are content to use what God has given them.
- Different stewards are given different talents and treasures.

3. Stewardship of your time.

- Good stewards manage their time to be efficient in doing more for the Lord.
- Good stewards know how to discern God's will.
- Good stewards discipline themselves to do well.
- Good stewards use goals to stay focused and do more.

4. Stewardship of your talents.

- Recognize your talents from God.
- Thank God for the talents you have.
- Pray for wisdom to use your talents.

5. Stewardship of your treasures.

- Loving money is sin.
- Learn how to use money and wealth for the Lord.
- Learn how to manage your finances well for the Lord.

6. Stewardship of relationships.

- The problem of anger.
- The roles of trust, reconciliation, and love in relationships.
- The importance of trust.
- The importance of repentance.
- The importance of forgiveness.
- The importance of love.

7. Living the abundant life.

- Jesus came to give abundant life.
- Abundant life is more than we could ever hope for.
- Abundant life begins with eternal life.
- Abundant life is a fulfilled life.
- Abundant life is a life of meaningfulness and greater purpose.

8. Teach others to be good stewards.

- Find someone interested in learning about being a good steward and disciple him/her for the Lord.
- Study stewardship together and be better disciples.
- Be consistent, trustworthy, and loving.

11

POINTS TO REMEMBER AND TO SHARE

1. Jesus wants us to invest our time, talents, and treasures for the purpose of winning souls and making disciples.
2. Good stewards are prepared for the Lord's return.
3. Christians will be judged for the investment choices they make.
4. Good stewards are thankful to God for the time, talents, and treasures they have.
5. Good stewards manage God's possessions.
6. Good stewards live for God, not for themselves.
7. Good stewards fulfill the first and great commandment.
8. Good stewards invest in others.
9. Good stewards invest their time, talents, and treasures for an increase in saved souls.
10. Good stewards are content.
11. Different stewards use different talents and treasures in different ways to achieve the same goal.
12. Good stewards set goals to be more effective.
13. Good stewards maintain their priorities.
14. Good stewards know how to determine God's will.

15. Good stewards are disciplined to overcome the resistance of their flesh.
16. Good stewards learn from stewards who are doing a good job.
17. Good stewards know what they are good at doing.
18. Good stewards do not compare their gifts to determine who is better.
19. Money is not evil, but it can be used for evil purposes.
20. The love of money is evil.
21. The love of money displaces God as a person's first love.
22. All that we have belongs to the Lord.
23. Everything we are stewards of should be used to fulfill God's purpose.
24. God expects us to invest a tenth of our earnings in His church.
25. Treasures are from God to use to increase the number of saved souls.
26. Increasing wealth to increase giving to God's ministries is not sin.
27. Health, wisdom, and diligence are essential to good stewardship of assets.
28. God gives wisdom so that stewards know the best way to invest their time, talent, and treasures.
29. Anger is evidence of not being under the control of the Spirit of God.
30. Trust, reconciliation, and love are essential for good relationships.
31. Trust is what others think about you.
32. Reconciliation is what good stewards strive to achieve.
33. Love is what good stewards show toward offenders.
34. Trust is essential for good relationships.
35. Repentance and forgiveness are essential for reconciliation.

36. Offenders are expected to apologize and give assurance of their trustworthiness.
37. Forgiveness can be conditional, based on whether the offender shows true repentance.
38. Forgiveness does not require trusting the offender or putting yourself at risk of being harmed.
39. A community of good stewards is wholesome and safe.
40. Love for God and others protects stewards from yielding to sin, resentment, and anger.
41. Love for God and others keeps you focused on your priority of reconciling souls to Christ.
42. Forgiveness is important for your spiritual well-being and for your ministry of reconciliation.
43. The abundant life is eternal life and peace with God, a life filled with purpose and heavenly treasures.
44. Good stewards learn how to win souls and train disciples.

ABOUT THE AUTHOR

Dr. Patrick Briney is the First Associate Pastor of Mission Blvd. Baptist Church. He is a missionary to academic communities and is an author, speaker, scientist, minister, and teacher of practical Christianity worldwide.

Blending professional training in science as a microbiologist who specialized in immunology and infectious diseases and over forty years of ministry experience as a missionary/pastor, Dr. Briney offers practical teaching relevant for anyone wanting to learn more about Jesus Christ, the Bible, discipleship, and creation science. Dr. Briney has created and led unique workshops for thousands of people globally.

Points Of Contact

Email: patrick@patrickbriney.com

Website: Visit https://patrickbriney.com, subscribe, and receive a free eBook

facebook.com/drpatrickbriney

twitter.com/drpatrickbriney

instagram.com/drpatrickbriney

linkedin.com/in/patrickbriney

More Resources

Visit https://lifechangingscriptures.org for more books and resources.

www.ingramcontent.com/pod-product-compliance
Lightning Source LLC
LaVergne TN
LVHW021405080426
835508LV00020B/2464